BIGGEST BOOK
OF
SCIENCE & SPACE

Text by
Amanda Ericson, Barbie Heit, Jane Parker Resnick, Rebecca L. Grambo, Tony Tallarico
Scientific Consultant
Jennifer Gresham—Director of Education, Zoo New England
Photo Credits
Dreamstime, iStockphoto

Kidsbooks®

Copyright © 2020 Kidsbooks, LLC
3535 West Peterson Avenue
Chicago, IL 60659

032001032GD
Printed in China

www.kidsbookspublishing.com

Get ready to learn about
the incredible world of

SCIENCE & SPACE!

Find out:

- **What household items can be used as compost in a garden**
- **Where the legend of the tooth fairy came from**
- **How scientists discover new planets**
- **What happened to the dinosaurs**
- **Fun facts about wacky weather, awesome astronauts, and cool critters**

And much, much more!

Also includes picture puzzles, mazes, word searches, and other fun activities.

Get ready to impress family and friends with your knowledge of science and space!

Kidsbooks®

So You Want to Be A Scientist

What does a chemist do?

Chemists study matter to understand how elements join together to form different substances. It's almost like taking apart the ingredients of a cake to see how the cake is made. Medical professionals, pharmacists, veterinarians, nurses, and dentists all rely on the work of chemists.

What does a botanist do?

A botanist studies everything there is to know about plants and their relationship to the environment and other living things. Botanists research and discover new species of plants, create new medicines, and uncover dangerous components of certain plants and vegetables.

What does an astronomer do?

Astronomers study planets and the sun in our solar system, as well as other stars, solar systems, and galaxies. They study the images they see in telescopes to make new discoveries about our universe.

What does a biologist do?

A biologist studies living things and their relationships to the environment. Biologists strive to make improvements in medicine, agriculture, and the industrial world.

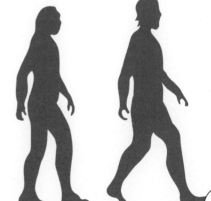

What does a zoologist do?

A zoologist is a biologist who either works directly with or focuses on the study of animals. Some zoologists work in zoos or wildlife reserves, while others work in lab-based environments.

WHAT DOES AN ARCHAEOLOGIST DO?

An archaeologist recovers and studies artifacts, old items left from early civilizations, such as graves, buildings, tools, and pottery. Archaeologists help us understand how people lived in earlier cultures and societies.

What does an anthropologist do?

The word "anthropology" comes from the Greek *anthropos*—"human"—and *logia*—"study." That is exactly what anthropologists do: study humans, from the beginning of time up to present day.

Deserts

Which insects build air-conditioned homes?

Termites. Inside a termite mound, hot air rises through the porous walls of the towering chimneys. There, carbon dioxide waste and heat escape to the outside, while oxygen comes in from the outside. The cooler, oxygenated air sinks into the mound, where the colony lives.

Why don't cacti have leaves?

Most plants rely on their leaves to make food, but a plant's water supply can evaporate quickly from a leaf's broad surface.

Cacti, which live mainly in areas where water is scarce, have no leaves. Instead, they make food in their stems. A cactus stem also acts as a water barrel, allowing some large cacti to store tons of water.

ARE ALL DESERTS HOT AND SANDY?

No. A desert is a place that gets fewer than 10 inches of rain a year, often much less. A desert can be hot and sandy, but it may also be rocky, dusty, or even very cold—as it is in Antarctica, for instance.

Why is xeriscaping a good idea in dry climates?

Xeriscaping (ZEER-uh-SKAPE-ing) is landscaping that doesn't require much water. Xeriscapers use plants that are suited for dry areas and water them with drip irrigation systems that lose much less water to evaporation than regular sprinklers do.

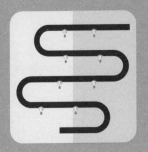

WHERE WOULD YOU LOOK FOR LIVING STONES?

In the South African desert. A living stone is a type of plant similar to a cactus. Each plant has two big, round, waxy leaves stuck together. The leaves, which are colored like pebbles, blend in with the plant's surroundings.

Tyrannosaurus rex

What was one of the largest meat-eating dinosaurs to live on land?

If you guessed *Tyrannosaurus rex* (*T. rex*), you're right! At 40 feet long and 20 feet tall, this massive dinosaur might have weighed as much as eight tons. That's heavier than three large hippos!

DID YOU KNOW?

Although *Tyrannosaurus rex* was one of the scariest dinosaurs around, it may not have moved very quickly. In fact, it may not have run at all! However, its size, combined with its strong sense of smell, excellent eyesight, and 60 long, sharp teeth made *T. rex* a great hunter.

The largest tooth found of a *T. rex* is 12 inches long.

T. rex **walked** on its **hind legs** and used its **long, heavy tail** for **balance.**

T. rex had a **huge** and **very heavy head,** but there were **holes** in it, so it could have been even **heavier.**

TYRANNOSAURUS REX
MEANS
"TYRANT LIZARD KING."

Thirty might not seem like "old age" to you, but for a dinosaur, it was considered almost ancient! Scientists can't always guess a dinosaur's age from its fossil remains, but they can sometimes tell the age of a dinosaur by the growth rings in its bones, kind of like the growth rings on a tree. Studies show that *T. rex* may have lived up to 30 years and in most cases likely died of old age.

Things That Go

THE PHYSICS OF A ROLLER COASTER

Roller coasters are fast and exciting! Most of all, they are fun. You might be surprised to learn that there are no complicated machines involved in making a roller coaster work. Instead, lots of science goes into creating this amazing amusement park ride—potential energy, kinetic energy, velocity, speed, friction, and gravity.

How do cars work?

Like a lot of people, you may rely on cars to take you places. Have you ever stopped to think about what makes a car go?

Most cars need gasoline pumped into their engines. When the ignition switch is turned on, the engine sucks in air and gasoline, providing power to the car and making the car go forward.

With the turn of the steering wheel, the car goes left, right, or straight. Stepping on the brakes slows down or stops the car.

The battery and alternator are part of the car's electric system. Without this system, you wouldn't be able to listen to the radio or turn on a light.

14

Animal Kingdom

Classifying Living Things

The **science** of **classifying** living **plants** and **animals** is called **taxonomy.** Using the system of taxonomy, biologists **identify, name,** and **group** organisms with others that **share** important **traits** so they can be **distinguished** from those that are **different.**

When you're having a regular conversation with friends or family, you most likely use "common names." You say your pet is a "dog" or a "cat," but scientists use different terms. Instead of "dog," they say,

"*Canis lupus familiaris.*"

SEVEN GROUPS OF TAXONOMY

The taxonomy of a dog, for example, looks like this:

Kingdom: Animalia

Phylum: Chordata

Class: Mammalia

Order: Carnivora

Family: Canidae

Genus: *Canis*

Species: *Canis lupus*

Subspecies: *C. l. familiaris*

Nature's Curiosities

Do woodpeckers get headaches?

You might think so, but the answer is no! Big neck muscles support the woodpecker's extra-thick skull, which acts like a built-in crash helmet to absorb the force of its hammering blows. The woodpecker also has stiff tail feathers, which it presses against the tree for support, lessening the impact.

What kind of bird lives underground and sometimes sounds like a rattlesnake?

The burrowing owl. This bird makes its home in the abandoned burrows of prairie dogs or ground squirrels. When threatened in its nest, a young burrowing owl puts its vocal organ to work. It doesn't sing; it makes a buzzing sound similar to the warning sound of a rattlesnake, another animal often found in such holes. A predator will hesitate before charging in on what it thinks is a rattler!

Why do some species of flower smell like rotting flesh?

To attract flies. Plants such as the giant *Rafflesia*, or stinking corpse lily, rely on flies for pollination. The flowers' stinky smell ensures plenty of flies show up to do the job.

WHAT IS THE DIFFERENCE BETWEEN A BILBY AND A BULBUL?

A bilby, also known as a rabbit-eared bandicoot, is an Australian marsupial with long, skinny ears, large hind legs, and a bushy tail. A bulbul is one of a family of rather plain-looking Asian and African birds. Bulbuls are busy, noisy birds that grow up to 11 inches long.

Can you get out of quicksand?

Yes, but not very easily. Quicksand looks solid, but it won't actually support a person's weight. If you sink into quicksand, the best thing to do is not panic. Thrashing about will only make you sink deeper. By moving slowly and carefully, however, you can work your way to solid ground. You can also float on your back, the same as on water, until someone can pull you free.

How do pythons, boas, and other constrictor snakes kill their prey?

By squeezing them to death—not by mashing them to a pulp. The snake wraps around its prey and squeezes a little tighter every time the prey breathes out. Eventually, the prey cannot breathe, and its heart stops.

Physics of Everyday Life

THE BIG PULL

Gravity is the force at the center of a planet that attracts other objects to it. Earth's force of gravity keeps our feet on the ground. Gravity actually holds the universe together, too. The sun's gravity keeps our planets in their orbits. Without it, Earth would shoot off in space.

Did you ever hear the saying, "What goes up must come down"? Try dropping a book. What happens? It comes down! Do you know why? If you guessed you're good at dropping things, you're partially correct. The other reason is gravity—the force that pulls objects down to Earth.

UP, UP, AND AWAY!

There are **four forces** that act on an airplane to get it up into the air and keep it flying: **thrust, lift, drag,** and **weight.**

When the **thrust** from the engine is **greater** than the force of **drag,** the airplane moves **forward.**

When the **forward** motion is enough to produce a force of **lift** that is **greater** than its **weight,** the airplane moves **upward.**

In order to remain in flight, the **thrust** must be **greater** than the **drag,** and the **lift** must be **greater** than the force of **gravity.**

Legend has it that Sir Isaac Newton discovered the law of gravity after an apple fell on his head. Newton, in fact, made many discoveries, such as the laws of motion, which explained the science behind aircraft—almost 300 years before the first airplane! The laws of motion would also form the basic principles of the study of physics. It's no wonder that he is often described as the father of modern science.

A Short History of Human Flight

1783

The Montgolfier brothers (France) build the first manned balloon. It is flown by Pilâtre de Rozier and the Marquis d'Arlandes.

1890s

Otto Lilienthal (Germany) flies and controls a hang glider.

1903

The Wright brothers (United States) make the first successful flight in a heavier-than-air machine.

1927

Charles Lindbergh (United States) makes the first solo flight across the Atlantic Ocean (from the United States to France).

1932

Amelia Earhart (United States) flies across the Atlantic Ocean from Newfoundland to Ireland.

1947

Chuck Yeager (United States) is the first to fly faster than the speed of sound.

1970

The largest passenger-carrying plane—the Boeing 747 jumbo jet—is launched. (It can carry up to 416 passengers, plus crew.)

Natural Wonders

WHERE is the LARGEST thing on Earth BUILT by LIVING BEINGS?
In the **sea** off the coast of **Australia. The Great Barrier Reef,** which is made of **coral,** is **1,250 miles long** and occupies about **80,000 square miles.**

How do male bowerbirds advertise for mates?

With decorated display sites called bowers. The male builds two parallel walls of sticks, which he may steal from another bird. Then he adds shells, pebbles, bits of glass—even buttons and coins. Blue feathers are the most popular items.

How do crickets sing?

By rubbing their wings together. One wing has a row of bumps that look like the teeth on a comb; the other wing is edged with tough tissue. When the toughened edge hits a bump, it makes a click that is amplified (made louder) by another part of a wing. Only male crickets sing.

Are humans the only animals that use tools?

No. Chimpanzees poke twigs into termite nests, then eat the insects that cling to the twigs when they are pulled out. Egyptian vultures drop stones on ostrich eggs to break them open. Otters balance stones on their bellies, using them to crack open clams and other shellfish. Other animals use tools, too.

What does the trap-door spider do with its trapdoor?

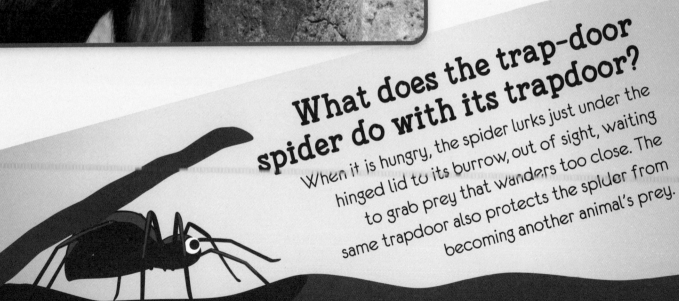

When it is hungry, the spider lurks just under the hinged lid to its burrow, out of sight, waiting to grab prey that wanders too close. The same trapdoor also protects the spider from becoming another animal's prey.

Solar System: The Planets

We live on a rocky planet known as Earth. Earth is part of our solar system, which includes the sun and its family of planets, asteroids, and comets—they all travel near or orbit the sun.

There are eight planets in our solar system. The sun's gravity pulls the planets. The closer the planet is to the sun, the faster it moves to keep its balance. Here are the planets in order, from closest to farthest from the sun: Mercury, Venus, Earth, Mars, Jupiter, Saturn, Uranus, Neptune.

VENUS
JUPITER
MERCURY
EARTH
MARS
SATURN
URANUS
NEPTUNE

You can play a memory game to help you remember the order of the planets. Take the first letter from each planet name—remember to keep the planets in order!—and use it to start a word in a sentence. Here's an example:

My Very Elegant Mother Just Served Us Noodles

The planets move around the sun in elliptical orbits. This means they follow a path shaped like a slightly flattened circle.

What about Pluto?

Pluto is freezing cold. On average, it's about 400 degrees below zero. The dwarf planet is so far away from Earth that scientists know very little about what it is like, but they believe it is covered with ice. Pluto is in a region where thousands of similar, small, icy objects are located. This is called the Kuiper (KY–per) Belt.

Word Search

Super Solar System

Pretend you are an astronomer and look for the planets and space-themed words in the puzzle below. Circle the words going across, up and down, and diagonally. Some words may be backward!

ASTEROIDS	JUPITER	NEPTUNE	SATURN
COMETS	MARS	ORBIT	SPACE
EARTH	MERCURY	PLANETS	URANUS
GRAVITY	MOON	PLUTO	VENUS

```
O Y Q T S S U H E E S Y C H G
R R Y V A D Y H N L G P T W U
B U H T C J I U A L R R A F J
I C U P H C T O Y C A I M C S
T R G T L P X S R E V A M A E
N E T T E A Y U J E I T Z Y M
B M S N S U N A R U T C S O O
B D U T A X W E S A Y S O U U
S H Q V E N U S T T O N A Q V
K Y Q A S M Q X O S E O O H Y
V K W D V B O I T R N Y R R P
J U P I T E R C U V C Q G O C
E N P W R V D X L S R A M U B
B S C S N M Y F P E D J Y J T
D B U J U R N V U W M J D I C
```

In the Air and On Land

Do trees live a very long time?

Some species do. Until recently, bristlecone pines in California were thought to be the oldest, living up to 5,000 years or more. Now super-old spruce trees in Sweden have been found. Some of the aboveground trunks of the trees are younger than the older sections, but the root system of the oldest discovered tree is over 9,550 years old!

WHAT FILLS THE SKIES OVER VERACRUZ, MEXICO, EACH AUTUMN?

Birds. Millions of raptors (birds of prey) pass over Veracruz as they migrate from their northern summer homes to wintering quarters in South America. Almost a million hawks could fly by in a single day.

HOW MANY ANTS ARE THERE ON EARTH?

No one has actually counted them, but scientists estimate that there are about

1,000,000,000,000,000

(that's one quadrillion!) ants on the planet. Anyone for a picnic?

HOW FAST DOES A SNAIL MOVE?

When a garden snail is really zipping along, it can manage 0.005 miles (26.4 feet) per hour. A snail crawls on its single foot. A special gland in the foot secretes mucus that lubricates its path.

HOW HIGH IS THE SKY?

The atmosphere is the air surrounding the earth. It is responsible for everything that we know as weather, from the most glorious of summer days to the most threatening of winter storms. Our atmosphere contains gases—nitrogen, ozone, methane, water vapor, oxygen, argon, and carbon dioxide. The air in which we live and breathe, the lowest and most dense layer of the atmosphere called the troposphere, is where all of our changing weather occurs.

EXOSPHERE
434 to 118,000 miles

EXOBASE
434 to 621 miles

THERMOSPHERE
50 to 434 miles

Aurora Borealis

Satellite

KARMAN LINE
62 miles

Hubble

MESOSPHERE
30 to 50 miles

Meteors

STRATOSPHERE
7 to 30 miles

Fighter Jet

OZONE LAYER
12 to 18 miles

High Altitude Balloon

TROPOSPHERE
0 to 7 miles

Balloon

Passenger Airplane

Plesiosaurus

PLESIOSAURUS HAD A VERY LONG, STRETCHY NECK.

Was *Plesiosaurus* able to bend its neck around corners to catch its prey? Yes. *Plesiosaurus* had 40 vertebrae in its neck to help it maneuver. Humans and giraffes only have seven!

DID YOU KNOW?

Instead of arms or legs, *Plesiosaurus* had four paddles. It used these paddles to swim through the ocean and move around on land.

Plesiosaurus did not lay eggs! *Plesiosaurus* gave birth to one live baby, kind of like modern whales and dolphins.

Word Search

Prehistoric Hunt

A paleontologist is a scientist who studies fossils and bones to learn about dinosaurs and other prehistoric life. Pretend you are a paleontologist and hunt for the following prehistoric creatures in the puzzle below. Circle the words going across, up and down, and diagonally. Some words may be backward!

ALLOSAURUS	MEGALOSAURUS	SPINOSAURUS
APATOSAURUS	MOSASAURUS	STEGOSAURUS
BRACHIOSAURUS	PLESIOSAURUS	TRICERATOPS
IGUANODON	PTERANODON	VELOCIRAPTOR

```
W A S T F H N S W B M S S I S
S F P U W N V P G H T U U G P
U P M A R J S I N E R U R U O
R D M R T U M N G U I R U A T
U N E M J O A O A Z D T A N A
A I F P Q P S S K D Z V S O R
S H K I Q A O A O U I J A D E
O T M G U I Y U U I X F S O C
L A T R S B E R O R H K O N I
A U U E P B J U A F U C M M R
G S L D Z Y B S I S E S A L T
E P V E L O C I R A P T O R F
M S A U R H S O R T E A S U B
G K T P T E R A N O D O N O M
N F T U S U R U A S O L L A N
```

Medical Developments

The Artificial Heart

American doctor Robert Jarvik designed the first artificial heart, the Jarvik-7, in 1982. Artificial hearts (like the one seen here) are implanted to keep patients alive while they wait for transplants or for lifetime use.

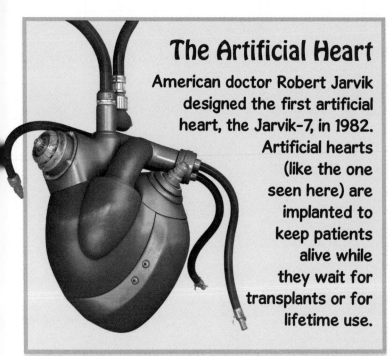

THE PACEMAKER

In 1950, a Canadian electrical engineer named John Hopps invented the world's first cardiac pacemaker, a device that is implanted in the chest to regulate heartbeats.

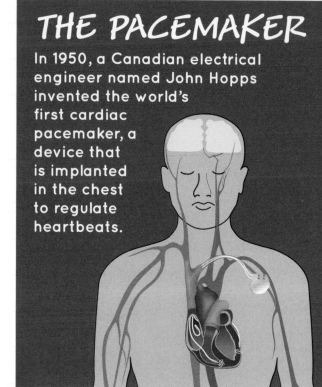

The Test-tube Baby

The world's first test-tube baby, Louise Joy Brown, was born in 1978. Patrick Steptoe and Robert Edwards, two British doctors, found a way to successfully fertilize an egg outside a woman's body. They performed in vitro—"in glass"—fertilization and Louise was born nine months later. In vitro fertilization is now responsible for bringing many babies into the world.

The 1964 Surgeon General's Warning

This report formally described tobacco use as a health hazard. It had an enormous effect on public policy and attitudes toward smoking.

A Plague in the Middle Ages

HAVE YOU EVER HEARD OF THE BLACK DEATH?

The Black Death was a disease that spread to humans through fleas and rodents, such as rats. It was a plague that lasted from 1328 through 1351, killing between 74 and 200 million people. It was called the Black Death because one symptom produced a blackening of the skin around swellings.

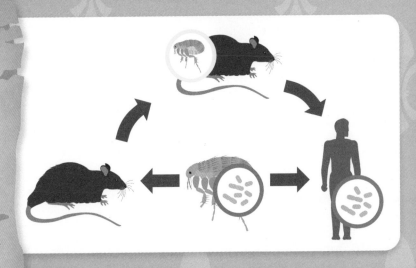

How were diseases like the Black Death treated in the Middle Ages?

Medicine in the 1300s was very limited. There were no antibiotics, so doctors made medicines from herbs and spices. They prepared drinks, washes, and ointments to help patients. Licorice was used to treat coughs, vinegar treated wounds, lavender and rose soothed headaches, and mint was used for poisonous bites.

How did the Black Death end?

Actually, it never really ended. People who were exposed to it died or became immune from exposure. It subsided over the years, but believe it or not, it's still around today. Today's victims, however, are much luckier. If the disease is diagnosed early, it is fairly easy to treat with modern medicine.

Under the Sea

WHAT DO DOLPHINS AND SOME BATS HAVE IN COMMON?

Both use echolocation to find their prey. They send out sound waves in the form of high-pitched shrieks, which bounce off objects. Returning echoes tell them the direction and distance of things they can't see. With echolocation, the greater horseshoe bat can catch moths in flight, and a dolphin can single out a fish from a whole school of them. Dolphins and some bats also use echolocation to help find their way around.

Can fish breathe underwater?

Yes. Water passes into a fish's mouth and over its gills. Blood flowing through the gills absorbs oxygen in the water. At the same time, the blood releases carbon dioxide, which is waste, into the water.

Where do pearls come from?

Pearls form when foreign matter, such as a piece of sand, gets inside the shell of an oyster or mussel, irritating the animal's soft body. To protect itself, the shellfish coats the object with layers of a smooth, hard substance called nacre. In time, as layers build up, the coated object becomes a pearl.

DOES ANYTHING LIVE IN THE DEAD SEA?

Not much, except for some specialized bacteria and plants. The Dead Sea is really a "terminal" lake—water flows into it, but none flows out. As water evaporates, it leaves behind the salt it contained. The water that is left get saltier and saltier. The Dead Sea is about eight times as salty as the Atlantic Ocean! By comparison, the Great Salt Lake in northern Utah is only three to five times as salty as the ocean.

How does a porcupine fish escape from its enemies?

By gulping water or air. The porcupine fish swells into a ball, and its normally flat-lying spines stick straight out. That makes the fish look too big and prickly for most predators to swallow.

How do coral reefs form?

A coral polyp is a tiny animal that builds a hard outer skeleton. When a polyp dies, it leaves behind its skeleton. Other polyps build on top of it, and still others grow on top of them. In warm, shallow seas over thousands of years, billions of these tiny skeletons form a coral reef.

Composting

Did you know you can make a beautiful garden out of compost and have fun while you're at it? It's true! Composting is nature's way of recycling. When organic waste such as leftover food, manure, and lawn mower trimmings break down outdoors, they turn into great fertilizer for soil.

You can make your
own composting bin!
Here's how:

1

Find a spot in your yard that is not too far from a hose or other source of water to set up your bin.

2

Find lots of brown stuff, like dead dried plant parts and pine needles. Brown stuff is full of carbon, which is needed for compost. Find lots of green stuff, like grass clippings, leftover vegetables, and weeds. Green stuff is high in nitrogen, another element needed for compost.

Spread a layer of brown stuff in your bin, about 5 or 6 inches thick. Next, add a thick layer of the green stuff. Sprinkle some soil over the mixture in the bin.

3

Water the layers and repeat the steps for each one until you have several layers in your bin.

4

In a few weeks, you might find new life in your compost bin. Look for earthworms, millipedes, and other insects.

5

When your compost turns into a very dark soil, it's ready to be used to fertilize your garden.

Making Compost

What can you use to make compost?
You may be surprised by some of these items:

Coffee grounds

Dog or cat fur

Hair from your hairbrush

Pencil shavings

Stale bread

Tea bags

Crumbs

Apple cores, moldy lettuce, or other old produce

Used tissues

Paper bags

Dryer lint

Dead houseplants and their soil

Nutshells (except for walnut shells, which can be toxic to plants)

Fun Facts about Stars

What is a star?
It is basically a big ball of gas and dust, or a "gust."

How are stars formed?
Stars are formed as **clouds** of **gas** and **dust** gather **together** after an **explosion** or **collision** in the solar system.

How old are stars?
Most stars are between **1** and **10 billion** years old!

The **SUN** is the closest **STAR** to Earth.

STARS COME IN DIFFERENT COLORS. HOT STARS GIVE OFF BLUE-WHITE LIGHT, WHILE COOL ONES GIVE OFF RED LIGHT.

WHAT MAKES STARS TWINKLE?

As the light we see from stars travels through the atmosphere closer to Earth, some of it bends slightly away due to movement of the air and disturbance in the atmosphere. That causes the twinkle!

DID YOU KNOW?

A black hole is what happens after a star collapses or after stellar collisions. A large amount of matter is packed into a very small space. The hole's gravitational field draws in everything around it. There is no possibility of escape.

This and That

What are atoms?

Tiny building blocks of matter. Every atom is made of some combination of protons, neutrons, and electrons. Atoms of similar structure make up elements such as oxygen, hydrogen, and helium. These are found in nature and often team up with other elements to form entirely new substances such as water. Two atoms of hydrogen and one atom of oxygen, for instance, make one molecule of water.

What is a nebula?

A gigantic cloud in space, made of gas and dust. A nebula can be dark or bright, depending on whether the particles it contains absorb light or reflect it. Some nebulae are bright because they contain hydrogen and helium gases, which glow. Scientists think that nebulae eventually condense to form stars.

What is solar wind?

Bits of atoms—electrons, protons, and some nuclei—that the sun's heat speeds up, until they are moving so fast that they escape from the sun's gravity and stream outward.

How does the sun make light?

By changing lots of hydrogen to helium. Incredibly high temperatures and pressures at the sun's center set off a fusion reaction: Four hydrogen atoms cram together to make one helium atom, but not all the hydrogen is used. Leftovers are converted to a form of heat and light energy that we call sunshine.

DID YOU KNOW?

A comet's tail always points away from the sun. That is because it is being pushed by solar winds!

What causes radioactivity?

Radioactivity is the energy given off by unstable atoms as they change to a more stable form. This energy can be in the form of heat or light. (The light may not be visible to the human eye.)

The Scientific Method

The scientific method is an organized way to figure something out by making observations and doing experiments. There are six basic steps to the process:

1 Ask a question. What do you want to learn? For example, maybe you want to find out if plants grow quicker with warm water or cold water.

2 Do research. Find out as much information as you can about your subject before you start experimenting. You may go to the library, do some Internet research, or interview people to gather information.

3 Construct a hypothesis. A hypothesis is a testable answer or explanation for your question. Based on your research, try to predict an answer or outcome to the problem. It would look something like this: "Plants must grow faster in warm water if cold temperatures cause leaves to turn brown."

4 Experiment. Do a test or procedure to find out if your hypothesis is right. To determine the growth of plants, water one plant with warm water, the other with cold water for two weeks.

5 Analyze your data. Record what happened during your experiment and use that as data. For the plant experiment, measure growth daily and write down your figures.

6 Conclusion. Review your data to see if your hypothesis is proved correct or incorrect.

Beach Life

People can't drink the seawater in the ocean, but seagulls can.

THE HORSESHOE CRAB GOT ITS NAME FROM ITS RESEMBLANCE TO A HORSESHOE.

Sea glass is made from old, broken bottles or other glass pieces. The glass is tossed around in waves and sand for so long that sharp edges turn soft and round.

Seaweed doesn't have roots. It grabs onto rocks to stay put.

Clams have rings on their shells. Just like your growth is measured in inches, the rings on a clam's shell show how much it has aged.

IF A SEA STAR LOSES ONE OF ITS RAYS, OR LEGS, A NEW ONE WILL START TO GROW RIGHT AWAY.

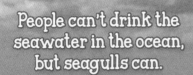

Blowing sand forms dunes that become homes to crabs, birds, rabbits, and mice.

A hermit crab doesn't have a shell. It finds an empty shell in the sand, then moves inside. When it outgrows the shell, it finds a new one.

Spit, Spot!

Which poisonous snake spits?

Africa's spitting cobra. It aims its venom at an enemy's eyes, sometimes shooting while still 10 feet away. The venom either immobilizes the cobra's prey or wards off a potential attacker. If the venom gets in a human's eyes, it causes burning and even temporary blindness.

Do vampire bats really suck blood?

No. Using its razor-sharp teeth, a vampire bat makes a small cut in its prey's skin. The bat licks blood as it oozes from the cut. A chemical in its saliva keeps blood from drying—and numbs skin so victims don't feel a thing. No, vampire bats don't attack humans!

How does the archerfish get its meals?

By spitting. This fish lurks underwater, watching for insects on overhanging leaves or grass growing just above the water. When the archerfish spots one, it spits a stream of water droplets, knocking the insect into the water where it can be gobbled up. The fish can shoot a stream 5 feet high!

WHAT DO SPITTING SPIDERS SPIT?

Something like glue. These spiders spray a sticky, gummy fluid all over their prey, rendering the victims immobile. Splat!

Why do snakes stick out their tongues?

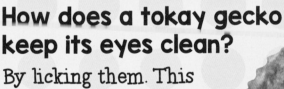

A snake's tongue picks up small particles from the air and ground, and carries them to two pits in the roof of the snake's mouth. Nerves in these pits carry smell and taste information about the particles into the snake's brain, helping identify its surroundings and track prey.

How does a tokay gecko keep its eyes clean?

By licking them. This reptile has no eyelids, so it uses its tongue to moisten and clean its eyes.

Mighty Mountains

Mountains make up one-fifth of the world's landscape.

Many people live on mountains.

There are mountains under the surface of the sea!

Alpine glaciers are commonly referred to as rivers of ice because of the way the ice masses descend from the mountains.

The highest mountain on Earth is Mount Everest. It is over 29,000 feet above sea level, and it's still growing! That is because tectonic plates are sliding and pushing the mountain up each year.

Plants found on mountains include conifer, oak, chestnut, maple, juniper, stonecrops, mosses, ferns, and climbers.

Groups of mountains together form mountain ranges.

MOUNTAINS ARE MADE BY THE CONSTANT MOVEMENT OF TECTONIC PLATES, HUGE SLABS OF ROCK, AT THE EARTH'S SURFACE.

Rock 'n' Roll

You've seen rocks everywhere, so you know they don't all look the same. Did you know they may have been made in different ways, too? There are three types of rock.

Sedimentary Rock

Sedimentary rock is a kind of rock that is formed from sand, mud, and, sometimes, tiny plants and animals. This is called sediment. It forms on the floors of rivers, seas, and lakes. Chalk is a sedimentary rock made up of shells of tiny animals!

IGNEOUS ROCK

Magma is a liquid that makes up Earth's crust. When it pours out onto Earth's surface, it is called lava. Lava usually erupts through a volcano. When it cools, it forms a kind of rock called igneous. Some igneous rocks contain valuable minerals, such as diamonds, gold, or copper. Pumice is an example of igneous rock. It is a lightweight rock that can float on water.

Metamorphic Rock

THIS KIND OF ROCK HAS HAD ITS STRUCTURE CHANGED BY HEAT OR HIGH PRESSURE. IT WAS ONCE SEDIMENTARY OR IGNEOUS ROCK, BUT THE MOVEMENT OF EARTH'S CRUST HAS CAUSED IT TO CHANGE. METAMORPHIC ROCK IS HARDER THAN THE ROCK THAT FORMED IT. MARBLE IS AN EXAMPLE OF METAMORPHIC ROCK. IT IS MADE FROM TRANSFORMED LIMESTONE.

Stegosaurus

Do you recognize this dinosaur with its armored plates? It's a *Stegosaurus*! *Stegosaurus* was not the smartest of dinosaurs. It had a small brain, only about the size of a walnut—one of the smallest of all dinosaurs.

THE PLATES ON *STEGOSAURUS* WERE NOT ATTACHED TO ITS BACKBONE; THEY WERE ATTACHED TO THE SKIN. PALEONTOLOGISTS STILL DON'T KNOW THE PURPOSE OF THE PLATES.

It's believed that *Stegosaurus* had one feature that not all dinosaurs had—cheeks.

A mother *Stegosaurus* laid eggs, and several babies hatched in her nest. At birth, the baby dinosaurs did not have plates on their backs. As they grew, plates developed, and the babies soon looked just like Mommy!

THE NAME *STEGOSAURUS* MEANS "ROOF LIZARD." ORIGINALLY, PALEONTOLOGISTS BELIEVED THE PLATES ON ITS BACK LAY FLAT, LIKE A ROOF.

THE **SPIKED** TAIL OF A *STEGOSAURUS* IS CALLED A **THAGOMIZER**.

DID YOU KNOW?

Stegosaurus was an herbivore. This means it did not eat meat like some other dinosaurs. It ate plants, along with small rocks to help mash up the plants in its stomach.

Fun Facts about Mercury

Mercury is the planet closest to the sun.

MERCURY ORBITS THE SUN ONCE EVERY 88 EARTH DAYS AT A SPEED OF 29.8 MILES PER SECOND.

Mercury is difficult to see from Earth because it is behind the sun. Just before sunrise and just after sunset are the only times the planet can be seen.

Mercury

The temperature range is so great on Mercury, there is no chance of life.

THE MOST **OBVIOUS** FEATURE ON MERCURY IS A **HOLE** CALLED THE

CAROLIS BASIN,

BORDERED BY

TALL MOUNTAINS
CALLED **SCARPS**

THAT CAN REACH HEIGHTS OF

1 MILE.

WHY ARE THERE SO MANY CRATERS ON MERCURY?

Mercury was probably hit by a lot of asteroids. Scientists believe that early volcanic activity may have shaped some of the planet, too.

This and That

HOW BIG IS THE GRAND CANYON?

About 7,000 feet (1⅓ miles) deep at its deepest point, 18 miles across at its widest point, and about 276 miles long.

TYPES OF TREES

There are more than 20,000 kinds of trees. Most belong to one of three groups: broad-leaved trees, conifers, and tropical trees.

CONIFERS, such as pine and spruce trees, are evergreen: Their leaves, called needles or scales, stay green all year. Conifers, which grow in colder climates, do not bear flowers.

TROPICAL TREES, such as palms, eucalyptus, and banyans, often produce flowers. They are canopy-shaped and have long, pointy leaves.

BROAD-LEAVED TREES, such as ash oak, are deciduous: They shed leaves in the fall. Their leaves are flat and wide. Some broad-leaved trees bear fruit.

Where does soil come from?

Soil is a mix of rotting plant and animal material, and bits of rock forming underlying bedrock. This mixes with the air and water to provide a home for bacteria, fungi, and tiny plants. There are three major types of soil: clay, silt, and sand. The bedrock determines the type, but climate, plants, and landscape also make a difference. Soil protects the roots of growing plants and carries nutrients they need in order to grow.

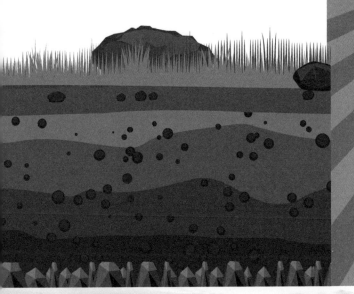

How do diamonds form?

Diamonds are made from carbon, the same element that makes up the graphite in pencil lead. Diamonds form in a kind of rock called kimberlite, about 75 miles below Earth's surface. The tremendous pressure there helps transform it into the crystals known as diamonds. Diamonds are the hardest known natural substance.

Will Niagara Falls always exist?

No. The falls exist now because a layer of hard rock called dolomite lies on top of the softer rocks, preventing the Niagara River from wearing them away quickly. As the soft rocks at the base of the falls wear away, the dolomite collapses, causing the falls to move slowly upstream. Eventually, over hundreds of thousands—perhaps millions—of years, the falls will disappear into Lake Erie.

Sea Creatures

A SEA HORSE is a fish that has the same shaped head as a horse. A sea horse swims upright. When it's time to rest, it will wrap its tail around a plant to stay put.

DID YOU KNOW?

Kitchen sponges used to be made from the skeletons of marine invertebrates. Natural sponges come in all shapes and colors and are found on coral reefs or sea beds. Left in the sun to dry, the soft parts rot away and a sponge is left with a soft skeleton made of protein— perfect for soaking up water. Now kitchen sponges are artificial, made by people in factories, but the principle is the same!

CRABS ARE CRUSTACEANS, WHICH MEANS THEY ARE AQUATIC ANIMALS WITH HARD SHELLS COVERING THEIR BODIES.

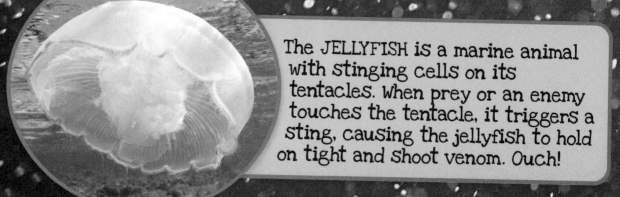

The JELLYFISH is a marine animal with stinging cells on its tentacles. When prey or an enemy touches the tentacle, it triggers a sting, causing the jellyfish to hold on tight and shoot venom. Ouch!

A DOLPHIN is a mammal that can swim long distances at a fast pace without getting tired!

BARNACLES are crustaceans that attach to solid objects, such as rocks and boat bottoms, as well as live animals, like shellfish, crabs, whales, or turtles. These sea creatures eat mostly plankton, microscopically small organisms, and they'll also eat any object that floats by and is small enough to be caught.

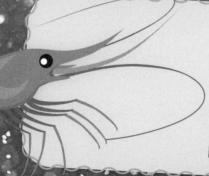

In addition to five pairs of walking legs, SHRIMP have swimming organs to help them move around in the ocean and freshwater areas. A shrimp's typical life span is between one and five years.

LOBSTERS have large pincers used for fighting other lobsters, catching fish, and tearing apart prey. Most of the time, however, lobsters feed on the remains of dead animals that fall to the bottom of the ocean rather than hunt live prey.

Fun Facts
about Venus

THE ATMOSPHERE ON VENUS IS MADE UP OF MOSTLY CARBON DIOXIDE AND NITROGEN.

Venus is completely dry and constantly covered by thick and heavy clouds. Because the cloud covering never breaks, we have not seen its surface from Earth.

VENUS IS THE SECOND PLANET FROM THE SUN. IT IS SOMETIMES CALLED EARTH'S TWIN, BECAUSE THEY ARE SIMILAR IN SIZE AND MASS.

Venus's DAYS are **LONGER** than its YEARS. One Venus day equals **243** Earth days, and one year is just over **224** days.

Venus

Venus is the **BRIGHTEST** planet in the sky, so it's pretty easy to find.

Many spacecraft have traveled to Venus. The *Venus Express* was sent by the European Space Agency, and it orbited Venus from April 2006 until 2014.

Venus rotates BACKWARD. All other planets, except Uranus, spin from west to east, but Venus's rotation is called RETROGRADE, meaning it moves from east to west. Astronomers don't know exactly why Venus rotates backward, but a large asteroid most likely slammed into it as it was forming, causing the planet to reverse rotation.

There are orange-colored rocks and dry dirt on Venus, as well as mountains, lava volcanoes, and highlands. There are only a few craters, most likely because Venus's surface temperature is so hot, asteroids burn up in the atmosphere before hitting the surface.

Venus is hundreds of degrees hotter than Earth. The average surface temperature is 900 degrees Fahrenheit (°F).

Rainbow Connection

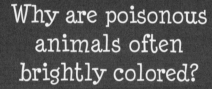

Why are poisonous animals often brightly colored?

Bright colors work like warning signs that say, "Keep off! I'm dangerous!" to potential predators. If an animal is lucky enough to survive eating or attacking one of these creatures, it will always remember that bright colors make for an unpleasant experience.

What makes flamingos pink?

Flamingos get their color from pigments in the food they eat, which includes small fish, insects, and algae. These are similar to pigments that tint carrots and tomatoes. Flamingos in zoos may turn white if they are not given the right kind of food.

How does a chameleon catch food?

With its long, lightning-fast tongue. A chameleon's tongue is as long as its body and tail combined, with a sticky pad at the end. When prey appears within striking distance, the tongue darts out, grabs the prey with the sticky pad, then snaps back into the chameleon's mouth—all in less than one second. Now that's fast food!

Are all white animals albinos?

No. True albino animals are white with pink eyes because they lack melanin. Other animals may be almost entirely white but still have melanin in some areas, such as their noses or eyes.

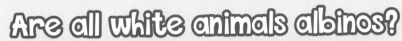

What makes some animals' eyes shine at night?

Animals that are active at night, such as cats, wolves, and owls, have a shiny layer at the backs of their eyes that reflects light upon the part of the eye where images are formed. This lets animals see in very low light. The shine that we see is light reflecting off that layer.

WHAT MAKES GRASS GREEN?

Chlorophyll, a bright-green substance found in leaves. Grass, trees, and other leaf-bearing plants use chlorophyll to turn sunlight into energy, in a process called photosynthesis. This is what provides plants with the food they need to grow.

Inside A Cave

Speleothems are rock formations in limestone caves caused when dripping water and dissolved gases leave behind calcium deposits.

THE TWISTY HELICTITES, ANOTHER ROCK FORMATION, WRAP IN ALL DIRECTIONS FROM THE CEILING, WALLS, AND FLOOR.

Caves don't start as caves; they form in rocks over millions of years. How does it happen? Specific types of rock—limestone, dolomite, gypsum, and marble, to name a few—can dissolve over time. These rocks wind up with large hollow areas and openings—and they're called caves. The formation of a cave is a very long, slow process.

THE SPIKE-LIKE STALACTITES AND STALAGMITES ARE THE MOST COMMON TYPES OF ROCK FORMATIONS. HERE'S A TRICK TO TELL WHICH IS WHICH: A STALACTITE (WITH A C) GROWS DOWN FROM THE CEILING, WHILE A STALAGMITE (WITH A G) GROWS UP FROM THE GROUND.

Fill-in Puzzle
Geology Genius

The word "crystal" comes from various root words, including the Greek *kryos* for "frost." Ancient peoples thought rock crystals were ice that was so frozen it would never thaw.

Use the words at the bottom of the page to fill in the blanks in the puzzle.

4 Letters
Sand
Lava
Gold

5 Letters
Magma
Stone
Slate

6 Letters
Pumice

7 Letters
Igneous
Volcano
Granite

8 Letters
Mountain
Sediment

11 Letters
Sedimentary
Metamorphic

For the Birds

Can you think of things that make birds different from other animals? Try and guess.

If you guessed they are the only animals to lay eggs, that's a good try, but not correct. Other animals—like fish, amphibians, reptiles, insects, and even some mammals—hatch from eggs, just like birds.

Now are you guessing they're the only type of animals that have beaks? That's another good guess, but not completely accurate. The duck-billed platypus is a mammal that has a beak, and so do turtles and some fish.

Maybe it's the pretty colors on a bird that make it different? No, other animals, like butterflies and fish, have bright, pretty colors, too.

Then it must be the wings! It seems like that guess would be right, but it's not. Insects have wings and so do some mammals, like bats.

Give up? The answer is
FEATHERS!

Birds are the only animals that have feathers. Feathers are made of keratin, just like your hair, skin, and nails. Most birds use their feathers for flying and steering. Feathers also keep them warm and help them hide from or attract other birds.

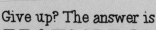

58

Besides feathers, these birds have other unique features.

PIGEON

Pigeons lay one to two eggs that hatch within 18 days. When a baby pigeon is born, it eats food that its parents have eaten and regurgitated (thrown up) because it can't swallow big food bites yet. Pigeons can nest almost anywhere and eat a wide variety of food, so they can live in cities where a lot of other birds can't.

Woodpecker

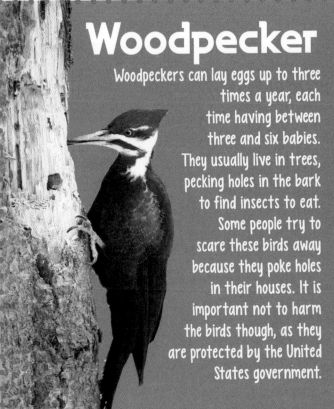

Woodpeckers can lay eggs up to three times a year, each time having between three and six babies. They usually live in trees, pecking holes in the bark to find insects to eat. Some people try to scare these birds away because they poke holes in their houses. It is important not to harm the birds though, as they are protected by the United States government.

Parrot

Though they are famous for talking and singing, parrots do not have vocal cords. They produce sound by pushing air out of their tracheae. Parrots are highly intelligent zygodactylous birds, meaning their first and fourth toes point backward while their second and third toes point forward.

Starling

These birds may produce two groups of offspring per year, each with four to seven babies. Starlings love seeds, but in the spring and summer, they look for baby insects to eat. Starlings swoop in big flocks and sometimes they get in the way of airplanes.

Velociraptor

Is that a dinosaur covered in feathers? Yes, it's a *Velociraptor*! In recent years, paleontologists have discovered that the *Velociraptor* was a feathered dinosaur. Even though the *Velociraptor* didn't fly, it had some things in common with birds: It laid eggs and probably tended to its nest like a bird.

THE CLAWS OF A *VELOCIRAPTOR* WERE AROUND 3 INCHES LONG.

DID YOU KNOW?

Paleontologists figured out that the *Velociraptor* was a smart dinosaur because they discovered it had a big brain relative to its skull size.

The *Velociraptor* was a **very fast** runner! It could run **25 miles per hour**—about the same **speed** cars travel on some streets.

THE *VELOCIRAPTOR'S* LONG TAIL HELPED IT BALANCE AS IT RAN, JUMPED, AND HUNTED.

Velociraptors had at least one retractable claw on each foot. They may have used their claws to catch and hold their prey.

Lunch Time

How is a snake able to swallow something larger than its head?

The top and bottom of a snake's jaw are held together with ligaments that stretch like rubber bands. The left and right halves of the lower jaw can spread apart, and the whole jaw can drop downward to open the snake's mouth really wide.

Do any plants eat meat?

Yes, but they gobble bugs, not humans. The Venus flytrap and other meat-eaters sprout traps that shut when insects trip them. Some trap prey with glue. Others drown insects in slippery-sloped water traps.

HOW DO HUMMINGBIRDS EAT ON THE FLY?

Hummingbirds survive on a high-sugar substance called nectar. To get it, a hummingbird sticks its long beak down inside a flower, then rolls its long tongue into a tube to suck up the nectar—all while batting its wings 50 to 75 times a second.

What do bats eat?

Most bats eat flying insects. Some catch fish, snare spiders and scorpions, or even feast on frogs, lizards, birds, and other bats. Fruit is a favorite with some bats, while others eat flower pollen and nectar. The vampire bat, of course, prefers only the blood of its prey.

When a sea star finds food, what does it do?

The sea star shoves its stomach outside its body and over the food. Then it eats and digests the food before pulling its stomach back inside. A sea star eats animals that move very slowly or tend to lie still, such as snails, clams, and oysters.

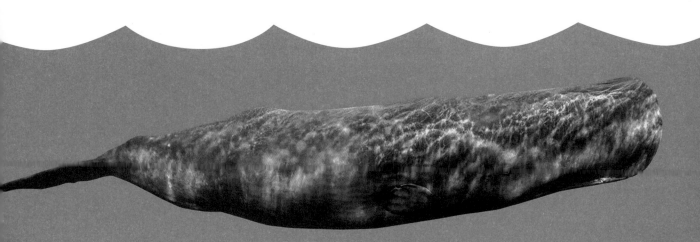

DO WHALES EAT BIG FISH?

Most toothed whales eat fish, but their diets vary. The sperm whale, for instance, mainly eats giant squid, but also fish, octopus, and skate, a relative of the stingray. The orca gobbles up seals, penguins, and other whales! Many other whales—in particular the huge blue whale—eat tiny shrimplike animals called krill. They certainly eat their fill of krill—up to 4 tons a day!

Photosynthesis

Photosynthesis is the process that plants use to make their own food, combining sunlight, carbon dioxide, and water.

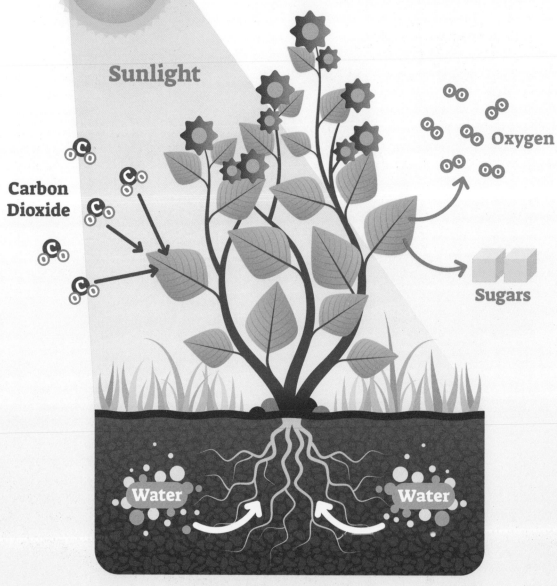

Sunlight

Carbon Dioxide

Oxygen

Sugars

Water   Water

Here's how it works:

1. ROOTS absorb WATER from the SOIL.

2. STEMS carry the WATER to the LEAVES.

3. CHLOROPHYLL uses the sun's energy to combine CARBON DIOXIDE from the AIR with the WATER from the SOIL, which are brought TOGETHER in the LEAVES in special UNITS called CHLOROPLASTS.

4. This produces SUGARS and STARCHES for the PLANT to use as FOOD.

5. OXYGEN is released into the AIR.

Easy Being Green

If you have houseplants at home, take notice of how they grow. The leaves of the plants are probably green. The green hue comes from the chemical chlorophyll.

DID YOU KNOW?

Living things that depend on other living things for food and energy are called heterotrophs.

Living things that produce their own food and energy are called autotrophs.

Why It Matters

The process of photosynthesis is extremely important for the existence of life on Earth. Humans and animals depend on vegetation for food. If plants didn't exist and thrive, neither would humans and animals.

Weather Report

Cumulus

Altostratus

Nimbostratus

What can looking at clouds tell us?

You can "read" clouds the same way you read books. Cloud shapes and sizes are clues to various kinds of weather. For instance, high, light, puffy clouds, called cumulus clouds, usually accompany good weather. Low, dark, heavy-looking clouds, called altostratus and nimbostratus clouds, are likely to signal a long, steady rain or snowfall. To learn more, keep your eyes on the sky!

If you like the sound of rain, where would be a good place to live?

You might try **Mawsynram, India:** An average of **467½ inches** of rain falls there every year! **Tutunendo, Colombia,** would be another choice; it gets about **463 inches** annually. **Cherrapunji, India,** holds the record for the most rain in a single time period (**192 inches** in 15 days); the most in one month (**366 inches**); and the most in one year (**1,042 inches**)!

What is hail?

Hail forms when water droplets are repeatedly swept upward into the cold parts of storm clouds where they freeze, then drop back down to pick up more moisture. It takes strong winds to keep hailstones circulating in storm clouds.

HOW BIG CAN HAILSTONES GET?

Are raindrops really shaped like teardrops?

No. No matter how often we see raindrops drawn that way, the real things look quite different. A raindrop looks more like a doughnut or bagel in which the hole doesn't go all the way through. The surface tension of water makes it take this shape.

Most are less than half an inch across, but some can be the size of softballs or larger. The largest hailstone on record, which fell in Bangladesh in 1986, weighed 2¼ pounds!

Earthly Greetings

THE GOLDEN RECORD

In 1977, NASA sent a "Golden Record" into space with the *Voyager 1* and *Voyager 2* spacecrafts. This record, made of gold-plated copper, contained images and sounds typical of life on Earth. That way, if other life forms in the universe discovered the record, they could get a glimpse of our world. The surface of the record contained this inscription, "To the makers of music—all worlds, all times."

The following examples of images, music, greetings, and sounds were included on the record.

Images

- Airplane
- Book
- Classroom
- Supermarket
- Fishing boat
- Astronaut
- Houses
- Traffic
- DNA structure
- Music score
- Seashore
- Crocodile
- Jane Goodall and chimpanzees
- Museum
- Factory
- Sunset

Music

- Aboriginal songs from Australia
- Percussion from Senegal
- *Shakuhachi* (a type of flute) from Japan
- Panpipes and drums from Peru
- "Johnny B. Goode" by Chuck Berry
- "Melancholy Blues" by Louis Armstrong
- Classical music by Bach, Beethoven, and Stravinsky

Greetings

Fifty-five speakers, all in different languages, chose their own unique greetings. Examples included:

- "Hi. How are you? Wish you peace, health and happiness."
- "Welcome, creatures from beyond the outer world."
- "Greetings to our friends in the stars. We wish that we will meet you someday."

Sounds
- Weather (wind, rain, thunder)
- Heartbeat
- Laughter
- Footsteps
- Animals (crickets, birds, frogs, dogs, chimpanzees, elephants)
- Transportation (train, bus, tractor, horse and cart, ships)

Create Your Own Golden Record

What things are important to you? What do you think best represents life on Earth as you know it? In each box below, write or draw an example of an image, a song or music style, a greeting, and a sound that you think would teach others about human life on our planet.

IMAGE	MUSIC
GREETING	SOUND

Destructive Winds

Did you know that TYPHOONS, CYCLONES, HURRICANES, and TORNADOES are some of nature's most powerful forces? They blow in a spiral of violent rainstorms and can have wind-speeds of over 75 miles per hour. In the Pacific Ocean, these powerful winds are called typhoons; in the Indian Ocean, they're called cyclones; in the North Atlantic, they're called hurricanes. Over land they are called tornadoes. Typhoons and cyclones are very similar to hurricanes. The only real difference between the storms is their geographic location.

How is a tornado measured?

With the Fujita tornado scale, developed in the late 1960s by Dr. T. Theodore Fujita, a tornado specialist. The scale has six levels:

Scale Number	Wind Speed	Damage Caused
F-0	Up to 72 mph	Light
F-1	73-112 mph	Moderate
F-2	113-157 mph	Considerable
F-3	158-206 mph	Severe
F-4	207-260 mph	Devastating
F-5	261-318 mph	Incredible

TORNADOES are violently destructive windstorms with wind speeds of up to 300 miles per hour. Although tornadoes pass in just a few minutes, they cause unbelievable destruction, sending people, trees, cars, and houses so high in the air, they fall with smashing force to the ground. Tornadoes are also called twisters and whirlwinds.

HURRICANES are huge storms that can spread across 600 miles and have strong spiraling winds of 74 to 200 miles per hour. When the storms hit land, the heavy rain, strong winds, storm surges, and large waves can cause great damage to buildings, trees, and cars.

Who started naming hurricanes?

For centuries, hurricanes in the Caribbean area were named for the saint's day when they struck. In the late 19th century, Clement Wragge, an Australian meteorologist, started giving hurricanes women's names. Since 1979, the names have been taken from an alphabetical list of both male and female names chosen each year by an international meteorological committee.

CYCLONES are tropical storms spiraling around a clear, central area called an eye. Only storms with winds higher than 74 miles per hour are called tropical cyclones. A tropical cyclone may be 600 miles across and carry hundreds of thunderstorms.

Recycling

Many items we use every day can be reused. Reusing, or making new things out of garbage, is what recycling is all about.

Why should we recycle?

It's good for the planet.

Recycling reduces the amount of garbage that takes up space in landfills.

It saves money.

We don't have to shop as often if we are reusing items.

It saves energy.

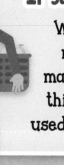

We don't have to manufacture as many products if the things we make are used more than once.

It's good for the environment.

Less trash helps keep air and water clean and prevents forest destruction. This protects wildlife and slows extinction.

Metal

Recycling **1 ton** of **aluminum** saves **hundreds** of feet of **landfill** space. **Aluminum** can be recycled from **cans, bicycles, computers, cookware, wires, cars, airplanes,** and other sources.

PAPER

Making **paper** from recycled material can reduce air pollution by **70%** and reduce water pollution by **30%**. Making recycled paper uses **30% to 55%** less energy than making paper from trees. Recycling **1 ton** of paper saves about **17 trees**!

THE NEWS

GLASS

Glass can be recycled over and over again—it never wears out! The energy saved by recycling one bottle can light a 100-watt light bulb for four hours, and a 60-watt CFL light bulb for eight hours.

PLASTIC

Americans use an average of 2½ million plastic bottles every hour, but only about 25% of these bottles are recycled. We save about 80% of energy when plastic is created from waste plastic (recycled) rather than when it's created from new material.

In the Deep Blue Sea

How large is the biggest fish?

The world's biggest fish is the whale shark. It grows up to 40 feet long or more and can weigh up to 33,000 pounds! It starts off small, though: A whale shark egg is about 12 inches long, 5½ inches wide, and 3 inches thick.

Is there a fish that uses a fishing rod?

Yes. The anglerfish uses one to do its fishing deep in the ocean. Growing from its forehead is a thin rod that ends in a glowing bump. The anglerfish sits still and jiggles that lure. Any fish that investigates the lure is quickly gulped down. Some anglerfish can even pull their lures close to their mouths for easier chomping!

What causes waves?

Usually, wind blowing over the water. The stronger the wind, or the bigger the stretch of water it blows over, the bigger the waves will be. Tides and earthquakes can also stir up water to make waves.

Whose eerie song might you hear in the ocean?

A humpback whale's. A humpback's song sounds like roars, squawks, and sighs to the human ear. A single song can last 30 minutes, and some parts are repeated—just like choruses in our songs. Songs sung by Atlantic humpback whales are different from those of their Pacific relatives.

What do grunion do at night on California beaches?

On certain spring and summer nights, grunion—a kind of small silvery fish—ride the waves onto the beach. Between waves, the females lay eggs in the sand and the males fertilize them. Then the fish ride the next wave out. The eggs hatch 15 days later, when there is another tide high enough to carry the young grunion away.

How much salt is in the ocean?

We don't know, exactly—but scientists estimate that if you took all the salt from the oceans and spread it evenly, it would form a 500-foot-thick layer over the entire Earth.

Space Firsts

Russia's *Sputnik 2* launched into space in 1958 carrying a dog named Laika. She was the first living creature to travel in space. Although she didn't survive, Laika made history!

© Olga Popova | Dreamstime.com

RUSSIAN COSMONAUT YURI GAGARIN WAS THE FIRST PERSON IN SPACE. HE TOOK OFF ON APRIL 12, 1961, AND WAS UP THERE FOR 108 MINUTES. BEFORE RETURNING, HE TRAVELED 17,560 MILES.

On March 18, 1965, Alexei Leonov stepped out into space from his spacecraft, the *Vokshod 2*, making him the first man to walk in space.

© Joni Hanebutt | Dreamstime.com

IN APRIL 1959, THE FIRST AMERICAN ASTRONAUTS WERE SELECTED BY NASA: SCOTT CARPENTER, GORDON COOPER, JOHN GLENN JR., VIRGIL "GUS" GRISSOM, WALTER SCHIRRA, ALAN SHEPARD JR., AND DEKE SLAYTON. THIS GROUP, KNOWN AS THE MERCURY 7, WAS CHOSEN OUT OF MORE THAN 500 CANDIDATES AND WAS MADE UP OF AIR FORCE, NAVY, AND MARINE CORPS TEST PILOTS.

Alan Shepard: First American in Space
USA
FOREVER
Mercury Project
UNITED STATES

Alan Shepard Jr. holds TWO important records: He was the FIRST AMERICAN in space, and it was on the SHORTEST spaceflight in history—only 15 minutes long!

The first American to orbit Earth was John Glenn Jr. He traveled in the *Friendship 7*, which took off on February 20, 1962, and stayed in orbit for five hours.

Virgil "Gus" Grissom and John Young were launched into space on the *Gemini 3* on March 23, 1965, making them the first two-person team in space. Their flight lasted five hours.

UNITED STATES

A few astronauts orbited the moon in the late 1960s, but Apollo 11 astronauts Neil Armstrong and Edwin "Buzz" Aldrin Jr. actually walked on its surface. On July 20, 1969, their capsule, the *Eagle*, landed on the moon while Michael Collins piloted the command module in space. Armstrong, pilot for Apollo 11, was the first person to set foot on the moon on an area called the Sea of Tranquility. Armstrong and Aldrin planted an American flag to mark the accomplishment.

© Forplayday | Dreamstime.com

Rockets

Thanks to space exploration, we know much more about our solar system today than we ever have before. Without our satellites or space capsules, space travel would be impossible. Without rockets, spacecraft wouldn't be able to launch at all.

When was the first rocket launched?

In 1926, a rocket engineer named Robert Goddard fired the first rocket propelled by liquid fuel. It reached a speed of 60 miles per hour and a height of 41 feet. It didn't reach orbit, but it was the first rocket to shoot straight up into space.

What happens when a space shuttle returns to Earth's atmosphere?

It's a hot moment. When the shuttle enters Earth's atmosphere, gravity takes hold and the surrounding air causes enormous friction. Friction causes heat. In this case, the fiery temperature is hotter than we can imagine—3,000°F. The shuttle is protected by special tiles on its underside. They are so good at shedding heat that they can be burning hot on one side and cool enough to touch on the other.

Crack the Code

Man on the Moon

Solve the cryptogram below to reveal what Neil Armstrong famously said on July 20, 1969, when he became the first human on the moon. Use the key below to fill in the blanks and reveal the quote.

1=A	5=W	9=E	13=M	17=D	21=X	25=R
2=B	6=V	10=L	14=Z	18=K	22=C	26=P
3=S	7=T	11=G	15=Y	19=I	23=Q	
4=J	8=F	12=O	16=H	20=N	24=U	

"
—— —— —— —— ——' —— —— —— —— —— —— —— ——
7 16 1 7 3   12 20 9   3 13 1 10 10

—— —— —— ——   —— —— ——   —— —— ——'
3 7 9 26   8 12 25   13 1 20

—— —— ——   —— —— —— —— ——   —— —— —— ——
12 20 9   11 19 1 20 7   10 9 1 26

—— —— ——   —— —— —— —— —— —— ——."
8 12 25   13 1 20 18 19 20 17

Neil Armstrong always loved to fly. He got his pilot's license at 16 years old, even before his driver's license! He went to college, served as a Navy pilot, and then worked for NASA as a test pilot—where he learned to fly over 200 different aircrafts. It's no wonder this career-flyer then acted as mission commander on Apollo 11: the first mission to the moon.

Triceratops

This dinosaur may have looked fierce with its body covered in armor and its three large, pointed horns, but it did not hunt other dinosaurs—it ate only plants. It had short legs and a very heavy body so it probably didn't move very fast.

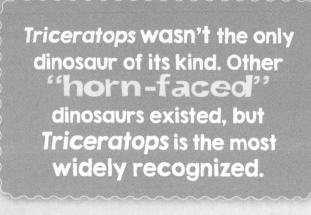

Triceratops wasn't the only dinosaur of its kind. Other "horn-faced" dinosaurs existed, but *Triceratops* is the most widely recognized.

Paleontologists are still not sure what the *Triceratops's* head frill was used for. It may have been used like a radiator to control body heat, or it may have protected the dinosaur's neck.

THE NAME *TRICERATOPS*
HORRIDUS MEANS
"THREE-HORNED FACE."

DID YOU KNOW?

Triceratops could have had anywhere from **400** to **800** teeth, stacked in columns.

Microscopes

Have you ever used a microscope?

There are different types of microscopes, but the optical microscope was the first invented and is still the best known.

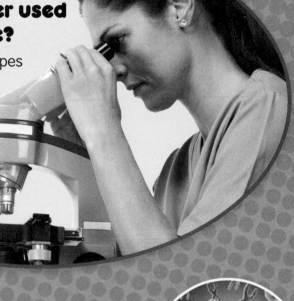

What exactly is an optical microscope?

It's an instrument with one or more magnifying lenses that uses light to inspect objects too small to be seen in detail by the human eye.

Eyepiece: lens that you look through.

Adjustment knob: moves the body tube up and down.

Arm: connects the top of the microscope to the base.

Body tube: connects the eyepiece lens to the objective lenses.

Objectives: lenses of varying powers of magnification.

Stage: platform to place slides.

Mirror: reflects light back up into the stage to illuminate slides.

How big do objects appear under a microscope?

The power of a microscope is usually displayed on the scope. For example, if you see "60x," that means the object you are viewing will appear 60 times its actual size.

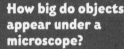

Why are microscopes so important to science?

Microscopes have been key in many scientific discoveries. For example, microscopes are used to check cells for diseases, such as cancer. They can be used to study details and structures of small objects, like the eye of an insect. They can also identify bacteria and viruses, helping scientists develop new vaccines and medications.

X-rays

When was the X-ray invented?

In 1895, Wilhelm Conrad Röntgen, a physicist in Germany, discovered X-rays while experimenting with vacuum tubes. He wasn't aware of the importance of his discovery: By the end of the decade, hospitals were using X-rays to take pictures called radiographs, which they used to examine bones and tissues.

How do X-rays work?

X-ray machines allow certain types of radiation—photons—to enter your body so the technician can take pictures. An X-ray is a quick and painless procedure that shows your bones in great detail.

Are X-rays dangerous?

Yes, exposure to X-ray radiation can be dangerous and cancer-causing, so radiographers (the people taking pictures) try to keep exposure to the patient to a minimum. If a doctor chooses to give a patient an X-ray, it is because he or she has decided an accurate diagnosis is more important than the risk of exposure to a small amount of radiation.

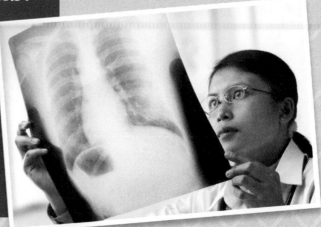

International Space Station

The International Space Station (ISS) was built by a partnership among 15 countries: the United States, Russia, Japan, Canada, and European countries (Belgium, Denmark, France, Germany, Italy, the Netherlands, Norway, Spain, Sweden, Switzerland, the United Kingdom).

A spacecraft could leave Earth and reach the ISS in around six hours—that's about the same as a direct airplane flight from New York City to Los Angeles!

The first crew to arrive at the ISS landed on November 2, 2000. The crew was made up of one NASA astronaut, Expedition 1 Commander Bill Shepherd, and two cosmonauts, Sergei Krikalev and Yuri Gidzenko. Since then, the ISS has been continuously occupied.

The ISS completes an orbit of Earth in about 90 minutes, traveling at a speed of 5 miles per second. In 24 hours, it makes 16 orbits of Earth—complete with 16 sunsets and sunrises.

THE CREW ON THE ISS IS GENERALLY MADE UP OF SIX ASTRONAUTS FROM DIFFERENT COUNTRIES.

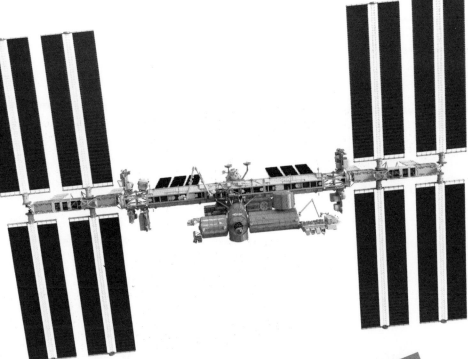

The spacecraft contains six sleeping quarters, two bathrooms, and a gym.

As of September 2019, there have been **239 visitors** to the ISS, from **19 different countries.** The **United States** and **Russia** have sent the **most** visitors, **151** and **47** respectively.

Since the ISS is the third-brightest object in the sky, NASA maintains a "Spot the Station" website where you can get updates on how to see the ISS as it passes over your area. To the human eye, it would look similar to a fast-moving airplane.

Over an estimated $100 BILLION has been spent on the ISS project.

THE ISS IS ALMOST THE SAME LENGTH AS A FULL FOOTBALL FIELD.

This and That

What happens along the US Continental Divide?

Water flows toward either the Atlantic Ocean or the Pacific Ocean. The Continental Divide is an imaginary line in the Rocky Mountains that marks where drainage changes from Pacific-bound rivers on the west side of the line, and Atlantic-bound rivers on the east.

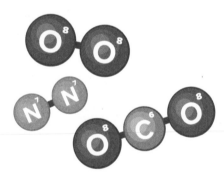

What made things rock in the United States near the end of 1811?

A series of earthquakes believed to be the strongest in US history shook things up in the area of New Madrid, Missouri, from mid-December 1811 to March 1812. The quakes rattled two thirds of the country, changed the course of the Mississippi River, and created new lakes!

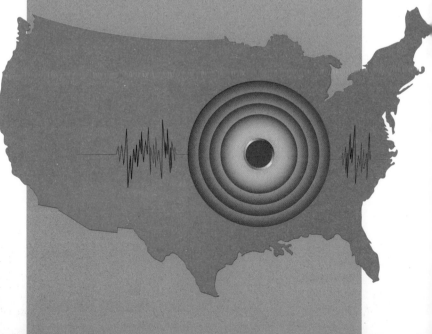

What is air made of?

Air is made of different gases. We can't see, smell, or taste air, but it contains the gases that we need in order to survive: oxygen, carbon dioxide, and nitrogen, among others. Human beings and other animals breathe in oxygen and use it to turn food into energy, then breathe out carbon dioxide and use it to make foods that help them grow—then they give off oxygen. What teamwork!

What is the San Andreas fault?

California's San Andreas fault is where two huge tectonic plates slide past each other. Hundreds of earthquakes occur here every day, most too small to be felt. During the devastating San Francisco earthquake of 1906, however, land at the San Andreas fault moved about 20 feet in a very short time! In all, there have been more than 160 major quakes in California in the last 100 years.

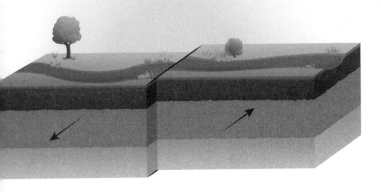

HOW DO HUMANS CHANGE THE AIR?

What humans do changes the air around us. Smoke from factories and exhaust from motor vehicles create smog (smoke + fog), which pollutes the air.

Where is the world's sunniest place?

The South Pole during summertime in the Antarctic. All that sunshine doesn't melt the snow and ice because the ice and snow reflect 50% to 90% of it right back into space. It doesn't get very warm there, either—it rarely reaches 32°F, even on a "hot" summer day.

The Five Dwarfs

Dwarf planets are round in shape, similar to the major planets in our solar system, and orbit only the sun. They are much smaller than the major planets but are too large to be classified into other categories. There are currently five officially recognized dwarf planets, but NASA believes there are many more waiting to be discovered.

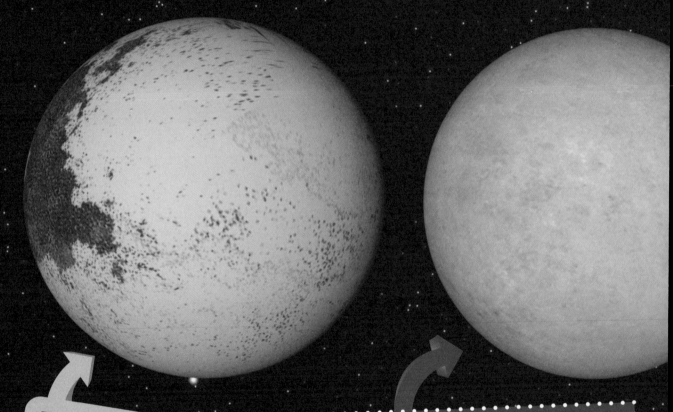

PLUTO

- IN 2015, A NASA SPACECRAFT TOOK THE FIRST CLOSE-UP IMAGES OF PLUTO.
- THIS DWARF PLANET HAS A GLACIER THE SIZE OF TEXAS AND OKLAHOMA.
- A YEAR ON PLUTO IS 248 YEARS ON EARTH.

Eris

- About the same size as Pluto, Eris is one of the largest known dwarf planets.
- One year on Eris is 557 years on Earth.
- Eris is three times as far from the sun as Pluto.
- According to NASA, the size difference between Eris and Earth is the same as a popcorn kernel to a nickel.

HAUMEA

- THIS DWARF PLANET IS THE SAME SIZE AS PLUTO.
- NAMED FOR THE HAWAIIAN GODDESS OF FERTILITY, HAUMEA'S TWO MOONS, NAMAKA AND HI'IAKA, ARE NAMED FOR THE GODDESS'S DAUGHTERS.
- HAUMEA IS ONE OF THE FASTEST LARGE OBJECTS IN OUR SOLAR SYSTEM, ROTATING AT SUCH A RAPID SPEED THAT THE CIRCULAR DWARF PLANET LOOKS LIKE THE SHAPE OF A FOOTBALL.

Ceres

- This is the only dwarf planet located in the inner solar system.
- Ceres is named after the Roman goddess of harvests and corn.
- According to NASA, the size difference between Ceres and Earth is the same as a poppy seed to a nickel.
- Discovered in 1801, Ceres was believed to be an asteroid until 2006, when scientists determined it was large enough to be considered a dwarf planet.

Makemake

- This dwarf planet was discovered in 2005 by scientists at Palomar Observatory in California.
- Makemake is important because it was one of two objects, along with Eris, that encouraged scientists to create the classification of dwarf planet.
- Makemake is named after the god of fertility and creator of humanity in the Rapa Nui mythology of Easter Island.

It's Cold Outside

What helps the little Arctic fox keep warm?

Its fur, for starters. Arctic fox fur insulates better than that of any other mammal. This fox's short legs, furry feet, and small, round ears help reduce the loss of heat from its body. The Arctic fox's body doesn't have to start working harder to keep it warm until the temperature drops below -40°F.

WHAT HAPPENED AT SILVER LAKE, COLORADO IN 1921?

It snowed **76 inches** in a single 24-hour period! It was not even winter then—that incredible snowfall occurred in the middle of April! Almost as bad was the 24-hour snowfall that hit Thompson Pass, Alaska, on December 29, 1955: 62 inches fell.

Why does snow sometimes SQUEAK?

When the temperature is 20°F or colder, soft, wet snowflakes turn into hard, rough ice crystals. The squeaking that you hear when you step on the snow is the sound of thousands of those crystals bumping into and sliding past each other.

What happens during an AVALANCHE?

Tons of snow slide down a steep slope. It takes very little to trigger an avalanche: a change of temperature, the weight of a new snow—even the weight of a single skier or the slam of a car door can set one off. An avalanche can move faster than 200 miles an hour, burying everything in its path.

WHAT ARE PINGOS?

Soil-covered mounds of ice found in permafrost areas in the Arctic and the interior of Alaska. A pingo is usually circular and may be up to 230 feet tall. At its center is a core of almost pure ice. In Eskimo, *pingo* means "small hill."

What kind of snow is best for making snowballs?

Snowflakes that form at temperatures close to freezing are bigger and wetter than those that form when temperatures are colder than freezing. Wetter snow is stickier than drier snow, so it makes better snowballs— and snowmen!

Spaced Out

What was the
SPACE RACE?

The Space Race was a contest of power between Russia and the United States. It began with Russia launching *Sputnik 1* in October 1957. The US *Explorer 1* was launched 119 days later, on January 31, 1958. The United States surpassed Russia in 1969 when an American walked on the moon.

© Alexander Mitr | Dreamstime.com

THE SECOND PERSON TO ORBIT THE EARTH WAS COSMONAUT GHERMAN TITOV, WHO TOOK THE JOURNEY ONE MONTH BEFORE HIS 26TH BIRTHDAY—MAKING HIM THE YOUNGEST PERSON EVER IN SPACE.

Cosmonaut Gennady Padalka holds the record for most time spent in space. Over the course of five spaceflights, he spent a total of 878 days in space—almost two and a half years!

In 1969, the crew on the Apollo 10 mission traveled **faster** than any human being has ever traveled—both before and since then. While traveling back to Earth, they hit a top speed of **24,791** miles per hour.

SCOTT KELLY IS THE AMERICAN ASTRONAUT WHO HAS SPENT THE MOST CONSECUTIVE DAYS IN SPACE. ON A 2015-2016 MISSION, HE WAS THERE FOR **340** DAYS IN A ROW.

During NASA's Apollo 17 mission, astronauts Harrison Schmitt and Eugene Cernan spent the most consecutive time on the moon's surface—around 75 hours. That's more than three days! Twenty-two of those hours were spent outside of the lunar module on three moonwalks to collect lunar samples.

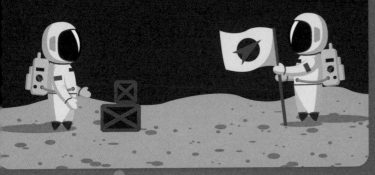

In 1998, American astronaut John Glenn Jr.—the first American to orbit Earth—flew on his second spaceflight, traveling on the space shuttle *Discovery* to become the oldest person in space ever at the age of 77.

THE LARGEST NUMBER OF PEOPLE IN SPACE AT THE SAME TIME WAS ACHIEVED IN 2009, WHEN THERE WERE 13 ASTRONAUTS AT THE INTERNATIONAL SPACE STATION. THIS NUMBER MAY INCREASE IN THE FUTURE AS SPACECRAFT DESIGNS CHANGE AND ARE ABLE TO TRANSPORT MORE PEOPLE AT ONCE.

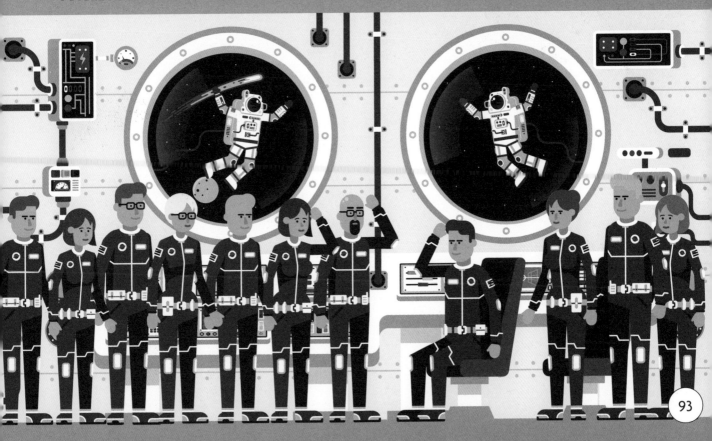

Famous Names

Dolly the Sheep

Dolly (a sheep like the one pictured here) was the most famous sheep in the world. She was the first successful mammal clone. Here's how it worked: The genetic material from Dolly's mother was taken from a single cell. Then it was transferred to the egg cell of another sheep. Five months later, Dolly was born as an identical copy of her mother. Dolly does not have a biological father. That's the idea behind cloning!

Dr. Christiaan Neethling Barnard

On December 3, 1967, Dr. Barnard, a South African surgeon, performed the very first human heart transplant. Unfortunately, the patient only lived for 18 days. He died of pneumonia, but his heart beat strongly until the very end.

ENG AND CHANG

Eng and Chang Bunker were conjoined twins born in the 1800s in Siam (modern-day Thailand). Conjoined twins are identical twins who are joined together by their bodies. Eng and Chang were connected at the chest, but their mother taught them to stand side by side by stretching their skin. They were husbands and fathers who lived and died together. The term "Siamese twins" originally referred to Eng and Chang, the first pair of conjoined twins recorded in medical history.

Dr. Jonas Salk

This medical researcher is best known for his discovery of the first successful polio vaccine. Up until the vaccine's development, polio was a major public health problem, killing thousands and leaving even more paralyzed. Children were most affected by the disease. Thanks to Dr. Salk's vaccine, polio is no longer a threat to humans.

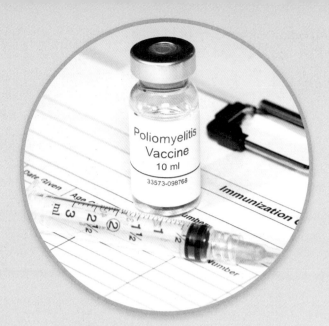

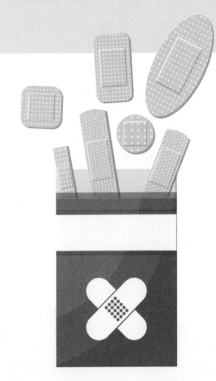

EARLE DICKSON

You can thank Earle Dickson for developing something you probably use often—the adhesive bandage. In 1920, Dickson wanted to help his wife who often cut or burned her fingers while cooking. He cut pieces of tape and put a piece of gauze in the middle. He then showed this to his employer, Johnson & Johnson. The company soon started producing these bandages under the Band-Aid® name. In 1924, the first machine-manufactured Band-Aids were made and boo-boos everywhere have been protected ever since!

Alexander Fleming

Back in 1928, Sir Alexander Fleming was a bacteriologist at London's St. Mary's Hospital when he observed bacteria being dissolved by blue-green mold. He experimented and found that a pure culture of the mold produced a substance—and that substance killed disease-causing bacteria. He named it penicillin. Today, penicillin is used to fight off infections, like strep throat, that might otherwise be very harmful.

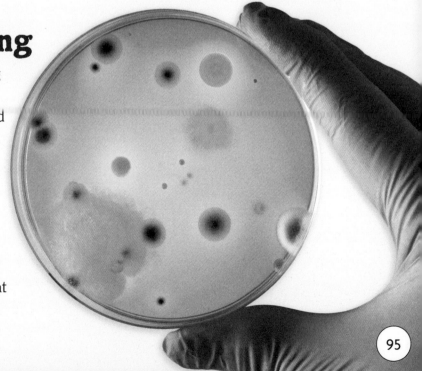

Lost in Space

What is the Milky Way?

Our home galaxy. We live in the Milky Way, a flat, spiral galaxy about 100,000 light-years across. Earth is located about 30,000 light-years from the galaxy's center. When we see the hazy band of light called the Milky Way in the night sky, we are seeing the edge of our galaxy.

Who named the constellations?

Ever since people first thought that they could recognize shapes in groups of stars, they have been naming those groups of stars, or constellations. Different cultures use different names for the same constellations. Most of the names that we use, such as Andromeda and Orion, are those of characters in Greek and Roman myths.

WHAT IS A SPACE STATION?

A space station is an orbiting spacecraft in which astronauts live and work for a long period of time. The Soviet Union launched the first space station, Salyut I, in 1971. It later launched six other Salyut stations. In 1986, the Soviet Union launched its Mir space station. In 1998, construction began in space on an International Space Station, and it was completed in 2011.

WHEN IS HALLEY'S COMET COMING BACK?

In the year 2061. The orbit of this famous comet, named after English astronomer Edmond Halley (see page 275), brings it close to the sun and Earth about every 76 years. Its last appearance was in 1986. American writer Mark Twain was born in 1835 when the comet was in the sky— and died in 1910 on the comet's next visit.

What is an eclipse?

There are two kinds of eclipses. A **LUNAR ECLIPSE** happens when Earth moves between the moon and the sun, casting Earth's shadow on the moon, which makes it seem to disappear. A **SOLAR ECLIPSE** occurs when the moon passes between Earth and the sun, blocking our view of the sun. The moon's shadow falls on Earth, making the sky dark during the day. For people inside that shadow, the sun seems to disappear.

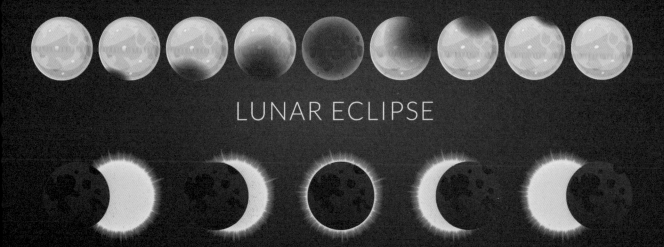

LUNAR ECLIPSE

SOLAR ECLIPSE

Burning Up

WHAT IS FIRE?

Fire is the heat and light created when things burn. Burning (also called combustion) occurs when oxygen combines with a combustible (burnable) substance, such as wood or kerosene, in a chemical reaction that produces a flame. For a fire to start, three things must be present: heat, fuel, and oxygen.

DANGER

Every year, fires take lives and damage homes and other property. Fires can spread quickly and easily. If a cigarette on the ground is not stamped out, it can ignite materials around it, erupting into a flame. Burning fragments can be carried by wind, causing other fires. Even the heat from flames can set surrounding materials on fire.

Fighting the Flames

When firefighters are alerted to a blaze, they speed to the site. First, they rescue people trapped in buildings. Then they use ladders, hoses, and other equipment to put out the fire. They wear special clothing and carry oxygen tanks as protection.

Since fires need oxygen to burn, they can be put out by taking oxygen away. Throwing sand on a campfire or tossing a blanket over a small fire can smother the flames.

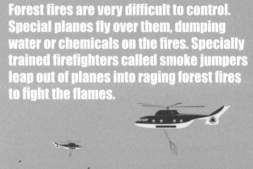

Forest fires are very difficult to control. Special planes fly over them, dumping water or chemicals on the fires. Specially trained firefighters called smoke jumpers leap out of planes into raging forest fires to fight the flames.

Crazy Maze
Velociraptor

Small and lightweight, *Velociraptor* was very fast. Sometimes known as the "speedy thief," this dinosaur could quickly steal food from other animals. *Velociraptor* is on the hunt for delicious eggs for breakfast. Help it find its way through the maze to find the nest.

START

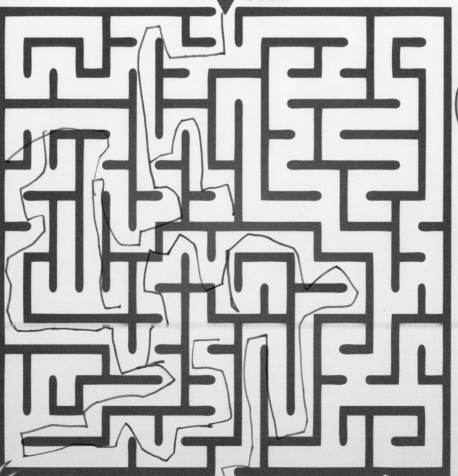

FINISH

The Circle of Life

Plants grow. They flower. They die. Then new plants grow again. Have you ever noticed this in the springtime? This is called a life cycle. All species, or groups of living things, have a life cycle.

Look at the life cycle of the cricket as an example. Have you ever noticed that you hear crickets at certain times of the year? Then they suddenly seem to disappear and come back again a year later? What happens?

1. First, the male cricket "sings" early in the fall. This attracts the female mate. Later, the female cricket lays her eggs in the soil.

Adult cricket

4. Little by little, the babies grow and change. By late summer, they are adults with wings. Female adult crickets will lay their eggs in the soil and start the life cycle again.

2. After the eggs are laid, the adult cricket may die, but in each egg a new cricket forms. All winter, the eggs stay in the soil.

Young cricket

Eggs

3. In the spring, the eggs hatch and tiny crickets are born. Each cricket has legs, eyes, and a mouth—but no wings yet.

What An Animal!

DOG-PADDLING

A polar bear can use its webbed paws to "dog-paddle" towards its prey. It can dive underwater for as long as 2 minutes, and launch itself as far as 8 feet into the air and land on the ice!

WHAT A SCREAM

With up to 120 members living in their group, chimps have to communicate. When they find food, they hoot, scream, and slap logs. Even young chimps can make as many as 32 different sounds.

SOUL MATES

Jackals often live in pairs of a male and female that stay together for life.

Seeing Straight

Like people, apes and monkeys have stereoscopic vision, which enables them to judge distances. That's very important if you're an acrobat like the black-and-white colobus monkey, leaping from one branch to another high above the ground.

How do you capture a skink? Not by grabbing its tail! Predators may be surprised to find that many skink species, including the fire skink, can break off their tails to escape!

Discovering New Planets

According to NASA, there are five main things scientists look for when searching for previously unknown exoplanets.

① Transit

The transit method has helped scientists discover 3,119 planets. When a planet passes in front of a star, it causes the star to appear dimmer because it blocks some of the star's light. Astronomers observe the dimming and use the information about how long the light changes, and in what areas, to estimate the size of the planet. The duration, or length of time, of the transit is also useful in determining how far away the planet is from the star—longer transit means a planet is farther away from its star.

② Radial Velocity

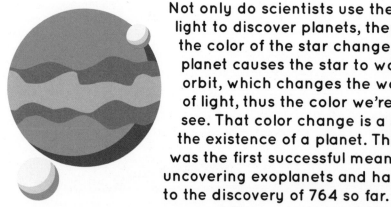

Not only do scientists use the dimming of a star's light to discover planets, they also record when the color of the star changes. The orbiting planet causes the star to wobble in its own orbit, which changes the wavelengths of light, thus the color we're able to see. That color change is a sign of the existence of a planet. This was the first successful means of uncovering exoplanets and has led to the discovery of 764 so far.

③ Gravitational Microlensing

Gravity is impacted by a planet's orbit, too. Objects that orbit, especially large ones, warp space and cause light to change direction or distort. Gravitational microlensing occurs when the gravity of a planet and the star bends the light to focus on another star, making it appear brighter. Then a kind of blip occurs because of the planet's orbit, like the way light bends when looking though a magnifying glass. This process takes place over the course of a month, but astronomers cannot entirely predict when it will happen.

④ Direct Imaging

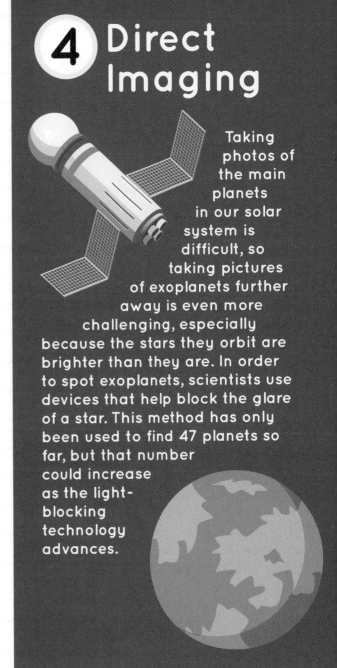

Taking photos of the main planets in our solar system is difficult, so taking pictures of exoplanets further away is even more challenging, especially because the stars they orbit are brighter than they are. In order to spot exoplanets, scientists use devices that help block the glare of a star. This method has only been used to find 47 planets so far, but that number could increase as the light-blocking technology advances.

⑤ Astrometry

This strategy involves tracking a wobble caused by a planet's orbit. Not only does the planet impact the wobble of the star, but that wobble can be visible when looking at the star's position in space overall. This method involves precise calculations, making it difficult for astronomers on Earth to achieve given their distance from the planets. So far, only one planet has been discovered using this method.

Exoplanet Exploration

WHAT IS AN EXOPLANET?

Unlike the planets in our solar system that orbit around our sun, an exoplanet is a planet that orbits around other stars outside our solar system. Spotting "wobbly" stars, or stars with an off-center orbit, is how scientists search for exoplanets.

EXOPLANETS ARE SIMILAR TO THE PLANETS IN OUR SOLAR SYSTEM. SOME ARE GASEOUS; SOME ARE ROCKY; AND SOME ARE ICY. HOWEVER, SCIENTISTS HAVE NOT YET DISCOVERED ANY THAT ARE SIMILAR TO EARTH AND COULD SUPPORT LIFE.

So far, NASA scientists have discovered around **4,000 exoplanets** and have detected another **3,000** that they continue to observe.

Neither humans nor robots have ever visited any exoplanets because of their distance from Earth.

In 1992, the first exoplanets were discovered. Then, in 1995, the first exoplanet that orbits a main-sequence star (a star that fuses atoms of hydrogen to form cores of helium atoms, like the sun) was discovered and named 51 Pegasi b. The planet is about half the size of Jupiter and is notable for how close it gets to the star, placing it in a class of planets scientists nicknamed "roasters."

The first multi-planet system outside of our solar system was discovered in 1999, when two groups of scientists at opposite ends of the United States independently discovered additional planets orbiting a star in the Pegasus constellation, bringing the total number of planets in that system to three.

The closest exoplanet to Earth, named Proxima Centauri b, is located about four light-years away. Even though it is the closest, it is still pretty far—the star it orbits, Proxima Centauri, is around 9,000 times farther away than Neptune.

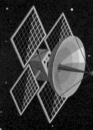

KEPLER WAS A SPACECRAFT SENT OUT IN 2009 TO LOOK FOR EXOPLANETS. TO DETECT THE EXOPLANETS, THE SPACECRAFT USED THE TRANSIT METHOD. KEPLER TRACKED THEM BY OBSERVING THE CHANGE IN A STAR'S BRIGHTNESS CAUSED BY THE EXOPLANET PASSING IN FRONT OF THE STAR.

The first planet Kepler discovered was the Kepler-10b, found in 2011. The planet is about 1.4 times the size of Earth and is exceptionally hot because of its proximity (nearness) to its star.

Women in Space

In 1963, **Valentina Tereshkova** became the **first woman** to go to space. She was a Russian cosmonaut who volunteered for her country's space program after fellow cosmonaut Yuri Gagarin became the first man in space in 1961. Selected from over 400 applicants, she piloted *Vostok 6* and orbited Earth 48 times, ultimately logging more than 70 hours in space.

© Alexander Mitr | Dreamstime.com

iStock.com/Roberto Galan

In 1977, NASA began accepting female applicants into the space program. Sally Ride, a California college student, was one of six women selected. In 1983, after her training in the astronaut corps, she became the first American woman to go to space. She was a mission specialist in charge of the robotic arm during a space shuttle mission that would help put satellites in space. She returned to space a second time in 1984.

NASA astronaut Mae Jemison became the **first African American woman** in space in 1992. Jemison traveled as a mission specialist on the space shuttle *Endeavor*—orbiting Earth 126 times—where she worked on research experiments involving bone cells. She logged over 190 hours in space.

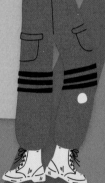

The success of the Hubble Space Telescope is thanks to Dr. Nancy Grace Roman, known as the "Mother of Hubble." She became NASA's first chief of astronomy during the 1960s, a time when women were not encouraged to pursue careers in science. Dr. Roman advocated for a space telescope back then, though it wasn't until three decades later, in 1990, that the telescope finally launched.

AS OF 2017, 59 WOMEN FROM NATIONS ALL ACROSS THE WORLD HAVE FLOWN IN SPACE, 50 OF WHOM HAVE BEEN FROM NASA.

As of 2019, the record for the most total days spent in space for an American astronaut is held by Peggy Whitson: a total of 665 days. She was also the first woman to serve as the commander of the International Space Station and the oldest woman to go into space, at age 56, during her 2016 mission.

On February 6, 2020, NASA astronaut CHRISTINA KOCH became the record holder for the LONGEST SINGLE SPACEFLIGHT by a WOMAN after spending 328 days in space—only 12 days shy of Scott Kelly's all-time 340-day record! She also performed the FIRST ALL-FEMALE SPACEWALK on October 18, 2019, with fellow NASA astronaut JESSICA MEIR.

Search & Find®
Laboratory

From Aristotle to Charles Darwin to Neil deGrasse Tyson, scientists over the centuries have used tools and equipment to conduct research and experiments in their laboratories. Even though modern labs rely on computer technology, some tools, like mortar and pestle, have been around since the Stone Age!

Search & Find® these 6 types of tools and equipment in the science laboratory below.

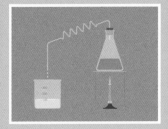

Bunsen burner

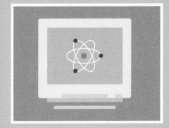

Computer

Mortar and pestle

Microscope

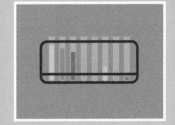

Test tubes

Scale

Answers on page 303

So You Want to Be an Astronaut

There are three main things NASA looks for in astronaut applications:

1. A college degree in mathematics, engineering, biology, physical science, or computer science

2. Useful job experience, such as piloting a jet aircraft

3. Passing the astronaut physical test (such as having 20/20 vision, though glasses are allowed)

Other skills that are important for NASA applications include speaking multiple languages, wilderness experience, or even scuba diving abilities. Nowadays you also must be between 62 to 75 inches tall.

In 1959, the first astronauts were chosen by the US military. At the time, astronauts had to be shorter than 5' 11" in order to fit into the spacecraft. Starting in 1964, NASA took over the process and looked for scientists who had doctorates in physics, chemistry, medicine, engineering, or biology.

If accepted into the NASA space program, candidates spend two years in a training period. Not everyone who makes it to the training period will be selected for a mission. Physical challenges include swimming laps and treading water—while wearing sneakers and a flight suit!

Clayton Anderson, a retired astronaut from Nebraska who spent a total of 167 days in space, applied to be an astronaut 15 times before finally getting accepted.

Today, all NASA astronauts are required to learn to speak RUSSIAN.

IN 2016, NASA RECEIVED OVER 18,300 APPLICATIONS TO BECOME AN ASTRONAUT.

Other countries have their own rules for becoming an astronaut. The European Space Agency recruits European citizens from countries like Sweden, France, and Italy. It's a hard job to get—in 2009, of the 8,413 best candidates, only six were selected to become astronauts.

Eye in the Sky

Launched in 1990, the Hubble Space Telescope is the largest telescope in space and takes precise pictures of stars, galaxies, and planets—making over 1 million observations.

The telescope is named after Edwin P. Hubble, an American astronomer who made some of his field's most important discoveries, including the existence of galaxies beyond the Milky Way.

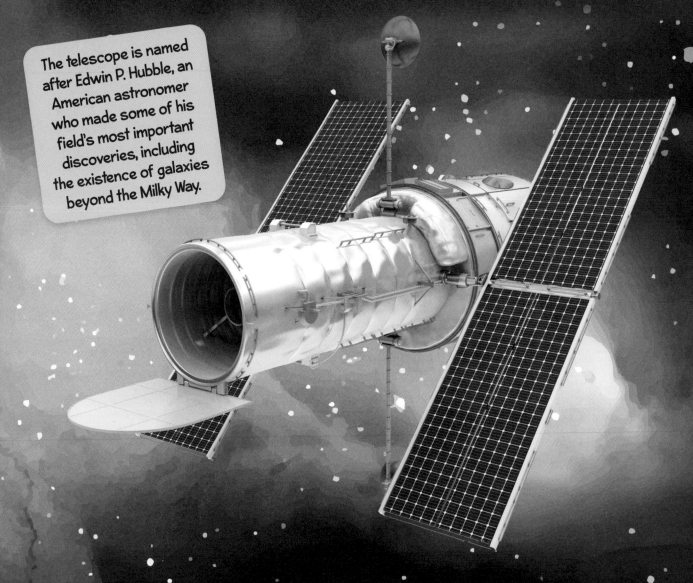

The Hubble only captures images in black and white. Scientists use lots of different filters to take multiple images of the same object in order to capture the different wavelengths, or colors, of light. Then astronomers make a composite (combination) of all the images to translate the object's wavelengths into colors that are visible to the human eye—creating the picture that is released to the public.

The Hubble Space Telescope is as heavy as two adult elephants and as long as a school bus. It travels around Earth at about 5 miles per second.

The telescope is solar powered but requires far less energy than you might think—just 2,100 watts of power on average. That's about the same as five refrigerators.

WHEN YOU USE A TELESCOPE ON EARTH AND LOOK UP INTO THE SKY, EARTH'S ATMOSPHERE IMPACTS THE LIGHT THAT COMES FROM SPACE. SINCE THE HUBBLE IS LOCATED ABOVE EARTH'S ATMOSPHERE, IT IS ABLE TO GLIMPSE PARTS OF SPACE PREVIOUSLY UNABLE TO BE CAPTURED.

Scientists believe the universe is almost 14 billion years old—which they were able to estimate due to crucial images taken by the Hubble which, so far, has been able to see 10 to 15 billion light-years away.

Want to take a look? The Hubble Space Telescope is open to anyone to apply to use, but competition is serious. The program accepts applications only once a year, and only about one-fifth of the hundreds of applications are given access.

In 2009, the last-ever mission to service the Hubble was completed. It will continue to be a tool for scientists and the public for as long as it works properly, as NASA has no plans to stop using it to explore the depths of our universe.

Drink Up

Did you ever wonder where your drinking water comes from? When you turn on your faucet and water streams out, it's coming from one of two places: surface water (like lakes, rivers, and reservoirs) or wells (that's groundwater).

WHY IS DRINKING WATER IMPORTANT?

All people, plants, and animals must drink water to stay healthy and alive. Water must be clean—germ and chemical-free—or it can make us sick.

How long can a person live without drinking water?

A person can live about one month without food, but they may only last three days without drinking water.

What is done to make sure drinking water stays clean in the United States?

The states protect our drinking water by helping farmers stop pesticides (chemicals that destroy pests) and fertilizers from getting into lakes, streams, rivers, and groundwater.

Water Shortage

As more and more people continue to live on our planet, more and more water is used. Though it may seem like the water supply is endless, there is danger that one day, there will be less usable water. Why?

DROUGHTS

Droughts are water shortages caused by lack of rain. This happens when winds shift and leave certain areas without rainfall for long periods of time. In some lands, droughts can be so severe, people and animals get sick or die.

Lack of Wells

We take our drinking water for granted, but there are some poor nations that cannot afford to provide it. Charities are sometimes set up to help these areas raise money to drill wells for clean, safe drinking water.

SPREADING DESERTS

When desert land spreads into the surrounding farmland, it is called desertification. Climate change is one cause, but desertification also happens when cattle and other animals overgraze, or when farmers burn vegetation. Without vegetation, land becomes very dry and can quickly turn into a desert area, with little or no water.

Forces of Nature

How do volcanoes cause colorful sunsets?

Volcanoes often pump large amounts of fine ash into the atmosphere. The ash increases the scattering of sunlight, spreading more red and orange light across the sky. This is especially noticeable at sunset and sunrise, when the sky becomes much more red and purple than usual.

HOW HARMFUL ARE TSUNAMIS?

An approaching tsunami may look less dangerous than it really is. In 1755, in Lisbon, Portugal, people went to gaze at the seafloor that had been exposed by a tsunami out at sea. Many were washed away soon after when the huge wave hit.

One of the most destructive tsunamis happened in Awa, Japan, in 1703, killing 100,000 people. In 2004, a tsunami devastated the shores of Indonesia, Thailand, Sri Lanka, and southeast India with waves of up to 100 feet, killing more than 200,000 people.

What caused a BIG BOOM in 1883?

The volcano of Krakatoa in Indonesia. Eruptions began on August 26, but the biggest explosion came the next day, when nearly the entire island was blown to bits. Steam and ash shot 22 miles into the air, and tsunamis sank ships and killed at least 36,000 people. People could hear the explosion almost 3,000 miles away.

Who were the first people to notice the island of Surtsey being born?

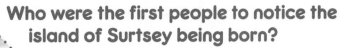

Fishermen. One day in 1963, they noticed something that looked like a rock in the ocean near Iceland where rocks had not been before. A volcano was erupting there, under the sea. As the lava spilled and cooled into rock, it piled higher and wider. Only four days after Iceland's brand-new island first poked out of the ocean, it was 200 feet high and 2,000 feet long! Today its diameter is 2,500 feet.

WHAT IS A GEYSER?

A hole in the ground from which steam, gas, and hot water spray into the air. Geysers occur in volcanic areas. Magma (melted rock from Earth's core) rises close to the surface, where it heats rocks. Those rocks heat water pooled underground. As that water reaches the boiling point, pressure builds until it shoots from the ground.

To the Backbone

Animals are separated into two main groups: vertebrates, animals with a backbone, and invertebrates, animals without a backbone.

Vertebrates

About 3% of animal species have a backbone. The five types of vertebrates are amphibians, fish, reptiles, birds, and mammals.

AMPHIBIANS were the first vertebrates to appear on land. They live both on land and in water (amphibians include frogs, toads, and salamanders).

FISH live in water, use gills to breathe, and are covered with scales or tiny, toothlike bumps.

REPTILES have scaly skin and lay eggs. Reptiles include lizards, snakes, and alligators.

BIRDS have no teeth, are covered with feathers, and have wings.

MAMMALS have fur or hair, use lungs to breathe, and feed their young with milk produced by the mother's body.

Invertebrates

Most animal species (about 97%) have no backbone. Some invertebrates have hard shells that protect their soft bodies—snails, clams, scallops, and abalone are some examples. Other invertebrates—insects, spiders, and crabs, for example—have tough outer skeletons (called exoskeletons) and flexible joints. Still others—such as jellyfish, octopus, and earthworms—have no shell or hard covering.

Vitamins

Foods rich in vitamins will help you stay healthy. These vitamins are known as essential vitamins because they should be part of your everyday diet.

VITAMIN B6
Great for your nervous and immune systems. Found in whole grain bread, liver, cereals, spinach, green beans, and bananas.

VITAMIN D
Needed for healthy bones and teeth. Sunlight, sunflower seeds, tuna, almonds, and oils are all good sources of vitamin D.

VITAMIN B2
Good for hair, nails, skin, and eyes. Cereal, eggs, milk, and almonds contain vitamin B2.

VITAMIN B3
Good for your brain and nervous system. Beef, chicken, tuna, peanut butter, barley, and bran are rich in vitamin B3.

VITAMIN K
Stops cuts and scrapes from bleeding by helping blood clot. Wheat bran, milk, liver, and green, leafy vegetables are foods rich with vitamin K.

VITAMIN B5
Helps you feel energetic and regulates your cholesterol levels. Sunflower seeds, broccoli, squash, and eggs are full of vitamin B5.

VITAMIN E
Helps scars to heal, great for the skin, and may protect against diseases. Peanut butter, oil, almonds, and sunflower seeds have vitamin E.

PEANUT BUTTER

VITAMIN A
Good for your eyes and vision, heart, lungs, and kidneys. Found in foods like carrots, fish, pumpkin, spinach, sweet potato, mango, and dairy products.

VITAMIN C
Important vitamin for healthy gums, bones, and cartilage. Citrus foods, kiwi, and green leafy vegetables are rich in vitamin C.

FOLATE
Important vitamin for unborn babies. Found in chickpeas, green leafy vegetables, nuts, and oat bran.

VITAMIN B1
Good for your muscles, heart, and nervous system. Found in whole grains, sunflower seeds, oatmeal, nuts, and lean meats.

Crossword Puzzle
Essential Vitamins

Complete the crossword using the clues below. For help, use the information you've learned about essential vitamins.

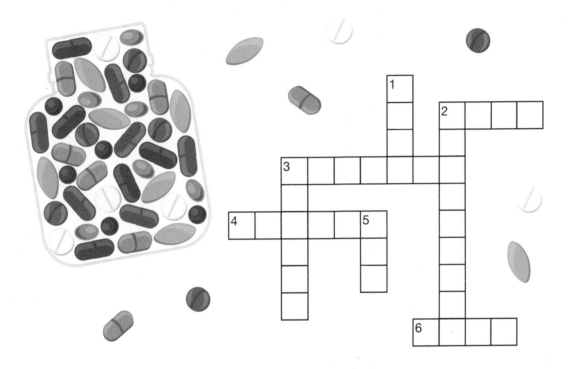

ACROSS

2. Eating carrots and other vegetables with vitamin A helps keep my _____ clear.

3. This orange food is a popular Halloween decoration and loaded with vitamin A.

4. Drinking a glass of _____ juice in the morning will give me vitamin C.

6. Raisin _____ is a cereal rich in vitamin B3.

DOWN

1. Drinking _____ may help my body to stop bleeding after a bad fall.

2. This is the fruit of a flower and very rich in vitamin E. _____ seed.

3. A _____ butter and jelly sandwich is yummy and packed with vitamin E.

5. An _____ and cheese sandwich is a good breakfast to provide vitamin B2.

Calling All Aspiring Astronomers

Telescopes are a useful tool to enhance your ability to see into space, but there is no need to buy one as a beginner. Humans have observed the sky long before telescopes! If you do want to take the next step, binoculars are an easy way to increase the details you see.

Whether you are in a busy urban center or a quiet town, here are some tips and tricks you can use to spot stars, planets, and galaxies!

The moon is interesting to observe, but a full moon can spread out too much light and make stars harder to see. It's often better to choose a night when the moon is not visible, or is in a crescent shape.

Do you know if you're looking at a planet or a star? Easy—a star twinkles, while a planet is smaller and gives off steady light. How about a shooting star?

If the moving light lasts only seconds, it is probably a shooting star. If the light is longer and steady, it's more likely a spacecraft, satellite, or even the International Space Station!

Do your research. Search online or head to the library to check out resources that can tell you when to spot different things based on the season. For example, meteor showers often occur in the fall, but the specific dates vary by year.

LOCATION AND WEATHER ARE IMPORTANT. THE BEST TIME TO STARGAZE IS ON A CRISP WINTER NIGHT, SO CHECK THE WEATHER FORECAST. HEIGHT ALSO MATTERS, ESPECIALLY IN CITIES WITH A LOT OF LIGHT POLLUTION, SO HEAD TO THE HIGHEST POINT IN YOUR AREA FOR THE BEST VIEWS.

There are many apps for phones that can help you identify the stars and constellations you spot, but printed star maps that you can make or buy work just as well.

Water You Looking At?

Why does still water act like a mirror?

All surfaces reflect light. If a surface is smooth and shiny, like still water or a mirror, the light is reflected in an even, orderly way, resulting in a clear image. If the surface is rough, the reflected rays are scattered in different directions, so we don't see a reflected image.

What makes a dry road look wet on a hot day?

Light. What looks like a puddle of water is actually a reflection of the sky. Light rays traveling through cooler air in the sky bend where they meet hot, moist air rising off the road. When light bends, it casts an image of the sky onto the road, just like a mirror.

HOW CAN A CAMEL GO SO LONG BETWEEN DRINKS?

A camel's body does a great job storing water. Camels don't sweat much, and their droppings are dry. A thirsty camel can drink 30 gallons of water in 10 minutes! They also get water from desert plants they eat. All liquid is stored in thick body tissues. When water is scarce, camels use the stored water—losing up to 40% of their weight.

WHAT IS HARD WATER?

Hard water has calcium, salts, magnesium salts, iron, and aluminum dissolved in it. The more dissolved minerals there are in water, the "harder" it is. The harder the water, the more soap you need to work up a lather. Too many minerals dissolved in water can make it taste bad, or be unsafe to drink.

How can water break rocks?

When water freezes, its molecules expand. If water gets into a crack in a rock, then turns to ice, it can widen the crack—or shatter the rock entirely. Over thousands of years, this process can turn huge mountains into hilly mounds of gravel. The pressure frozen water exerts on a rock is equal to that of an elephant standing on a postage stamp!

Where is most of the fresh water on Earth?

The ice sheet of Antarctica holds 80% to 90% of Earth's fresh water—frozen solid. That ice sheet is an average of 7,100 feet thick! (At its thickest point, it is 3 miles deep!) If it ever melted, the sea level around the world would rise by 180 to 200 feet.

Comets

Is it a bird?
A plane?
A UFO?

Have you ever seen a long, bright taillike figure soaring through the sky and wondered what it was? Most likely, it was a comet. A comet is just a lump of ice and rock traveling from the far outer solar system to orbit the sun. As it nears the sun, its ice melts, sending off jets of gas and clouds of dusty rock particles. From where we are on Earth, the dust appears to be a shiny tail stretching for miles.

A **comet** discovered in 1772 **reappeared** in 1826 and was named **Biela's Comet.** In 1845 it returned as **two** comets!

DID YOU KNOW?

Comets are leftovers from the start of the solar system. They often come out from near Pluto or a region called the Oort Cloud. The gravitational effect of passing stars pulls comets toward the sun, so they shine briefly in our sky.

What's the difference between a comet and a shooting star?

Shooting stars are meteors that burn up in Earth's atmosphere. Comets consist of mostly frozen gas, ice, and dust. Unlike planets, neither circle the sun, but they do orbit in space. Comets have fiery tails, which we see when they pass the earth.

Total Eclipse

There are billions of stars in the sky, and our sun is one of them!

The SUN is the LARGEST object in the SOLAR SYSTEM. It's over 100 TIMES LARGER than EARTH.

EVERY PLANET IN THE SOLAR SYSTEM REVOLVES AROUND

THE SUN

Every living thing on Earth depends on the sun to stay alive.

THE SUN LOOKS MUCH LARGER THAN OTHER STARS BECAUSE IT IS SO CLOSE TO EARTH.

How often can we see an eclipse of the sun?

Solar eclipses can be seen only from certain parts of Earth's surface— different places at different times. If you're willing to travel, however, the average number of eclipses is two to five times a year. Five is highly unusual. The last time Earth experienced five solar eclipses in a year was 1935; it won't happen again until 2206!

Earthquakes

An earthquake is a sudden shaking and vibration in Earth's surface.

What causes an earthquake?

There are plates along the surface of Earth that push against one another, creating pressure. When they slip quickly past after being stuck, pressure is released through surface waves—an earthquake!

Epicenter

EARTHQUAKES CAN HAPPEN **ANYWHERE**. IN THE **UNITED STATES**, THE **WEST COAST** IS **MOST** AT RISK, BUT **EARTHQUAKES CAN** HAPPEN IN THE **MIDWEST** AND ALONG THE **EAST COAST**.

About 80% of the world's earthquakes take place around the massive Pacific Plate, an area known as the Pacific Rim of Fire, which stretches from South America to New Zealand.

Do earthquakes always cause mass destruction?

Most often you'll just feel a bit of trembling for a few seconds during an earthquake. Sometimes, though, there is enough movement to really shake the ground, and the earthquake is strong enough to knock down tall buildings and crack huge trees in half. There is no known way to prevent earthquakes, but it is possible to lessen their impact by building structures designed to withstand earthquake damage and educating people on safety.

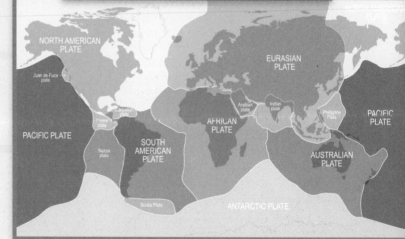

NORTH AMERICAN PLATE

Juan de Fuca plate

EURASIAN PLATE

Caribbean plate

Cocos plate

Arabian plate

Indian plate

Philippine Plate

PACIFIC PLATE

AFRICAN PLATE

PACIFIC PLATE

Nazca plate

SOUTH AMERICAN PLATE

AUSTRALIAN PLATE

Scotia Plate

ANTARCTIC PLATE

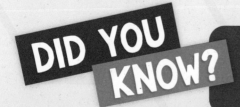

DID YOU KNOW? Up to 1 million earthquakes occur each year all around the world.

What is the Richter scale?

The Richter scale is a numerical rating of the power of earthquakes. It is based on waves recorded by an instrument called a seismograph. As each number goes up on the scale, the power is increased by 10. For example, a level two earthquake would be 10 times more powerful than a level one. The diagram below describes the effect of each type of earthquake on the Richter scale.

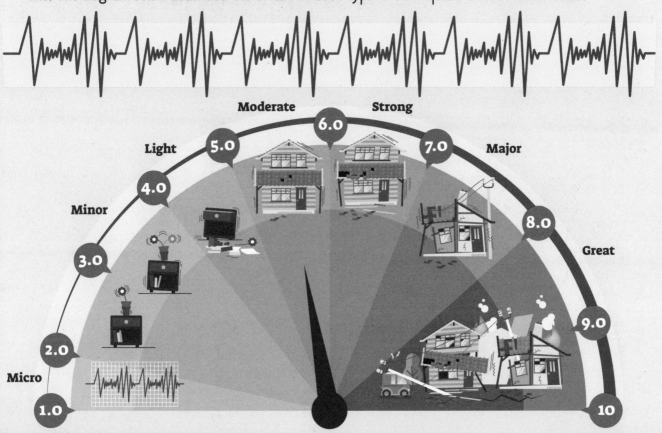

Number	Effect
2.0 or less	A very minor earthquake that cannot be felt.
2.1 – 3.9	An earthquake that still may not be felt. (Although a quake at the higher end of the range may be felt slightly.) These can cause minor damage.
4.0 – 4.9	A light earthquake that can be felt as general shaking but usually only causes minor damage.
5.0 – 5.9	A moderate earthquake that can cause damage to structures. Dishes, windows, and other fragile items may break.
6.0 – 6.9	A strong earthquake. It can cause major damage, especially to areas where large amounts of people live. Heavy furniture may shift.
7.0 – 7.9	A very major earthquake that causes serious destruction.
8.0 – 9.9	An extremely destructive earthquake that can completely destroy entire communities. Buildings can collapse in a level 8.0 quake.

The earthquake that hit the Tohoku region of Japan on March 11, 2011, was a 9.0 on the Richter scale. It killed over 15,000 people. The most powerful earthquake ever recorded on Earth was in Valdivia, Chile, in 1960. On the Richter scale, it was a 9.5.

Forest for the Trees

HOW DO FOREST FIRES START?

Often with a lightning strike. The air at a lightning bolt's center is very hot—as much as five times as hot as the surface of the sun. When that heat meets the wood of a dry tree, it sparks a fire that spreads to other trees. Forest fires are also started by careless campers who fail to put out their fires properly.

Was there really a man called Johnny Appleseed?

Yes. His real name was John Chapman (1774-1845). He traveled throughout the US Midwest, planting apple orchards. He also gave seeds and young trees to pioneers who were headed west, encouraging them to plant their own orchards. By the time he died, he owned many plant nurseries and orchards and had won fame for starting many others.

WHY ARE RAIN FORESTS SO IMPORTANT?

They provide homes for more than half of the known (and unknown) plant and animal species on Earth—more than any other habitat. Rain forests are abundant in medicinal plants and rid the air of pollutants, but, sadly, humans have cut down much of the forests. Today the forests cover only 2% of Earth's surface; once, they covered twice that area. Rain forests are in Central and South America, West and Central Africa, and Southeast Asia.

HOW TALL IS THE WORLD'S TALLEST LIVING TREE?

A giant redwood in California's Redwood National Park is the tallest tree on Earth. How tall is it? You could look out the top-floor window of a building 35 stories high—and still not see the top. Discovered in the summer of 2006, the tree, named Hyperion, is a whopping 379 feet tall!

Where was the First national park?

In an area that spreads across parts of Idaho, Montana, and Wyoming. In 1872, President Ulysses S. Grant and the US Congress made this area, named Yellowstone National Park, the first national park in the United States—and in the world. Today, the US National Park Service oversees 54 national parks, as well as a number of historic sites, seashores, memorials, and other protected sites.

Who was Smokey the Bear?

At first, he was just a cartoon character that told people, "Only you can prevent forest fires." Then, in 1950, a firefighting crew in New Mexico rescued a bear cub from a forest fire. Named Smokey after the cartoon, he lived at the National Zoo in Washington, DC, serving as a symbol for fire prevention. Smokey died in 1976.

DID YOU KNOW?

Fish scales are like tree trunks! Both grow more in spring and summer than in winter. This seasonal growth can be used to calculate fish ages. Fine ridges on the scales are closer in lean years, farther apart in years of abundant food.

Creepy-Crawlies

How many kinds of insects are there?

We know of about 5 million living species, but there are probably many more that haven't been discovered yet. However, habitat destruction, especially of the rain forests, is wiping out many species before we have a chance to learn about them or even know that they exist.

Which insect flies the fastest?

The dragonfly. When a dragonfly comes by, duck! It can travel as fast as 30 miles per hour. However, compared to many insects, this big bug beats its wings slowly—only about 25 to 40 beats per second. When a tiny mosquito takes off, it beats its wings (buzzzz!) about 600 beats per second, but only travels about 1 mile per hour.

Zebra caterpillars, as you might guess, have alternating black-and-white stripes, just like a zebra.

LADYBUGS ARE SPOTTED BEETLES THAT EAT OTHER INSECTS AND PLANTS. SOME PEOPLE THINK THEY BRING GOOD LUCK.

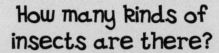

Why are some insects born without a mouth?

Because they don't need one! Some male moths live only long enough to mate before dying. They don't have a mouth because eating would waste the precious time they have to further their species.

WHY DO HONEYBEES DANCE?

To pass the word about food: The dance is a form of sign language. A bee that discovers a food source returns to the hive and dances, moving around and wiggling its rear end. Those movements tell other bees the direction and distance of their next meal.

Which is stronger, spiderweb silk or steel?

Spiderweb silk! You have to pull harder to break a strand of silk than you do to break a steel wire of the same thickness.

Suit Up!

Space suits help keep astronauts safe in many different ways. The suits help with extreme temperatures, hold water to drink, and give the astronauts oxygen. They also protect astronauts from space dust, which can move at speeds faster than a bullet.

NASA's first space suits, designed for the Mercury program, could only be worn inside the spacecraft. For the Gemini program, NASA developed space suits that allowed astronauts to go on spacewalks. Though not as complex as space suits today, the Gemini versions included oxygen hoses connected to the spacecraft.

A space suit used in the International Space Station is officially called an EMU, or Extravehicular Mobility Unit. This means it is designed to be used outside the spacecraft in space.

DURING THE APOLLO MISSION, BEFORE AN ASTRONAUT PUT ON A SPACE SUIT, THE SUIT WAS X-RAYED AT LEAST TWICE TO MAKE SURE THERE WERE NO PINS FROM THE TAILORS AND SEAMSTRESSES.

The backpack an astronaut wears performs many jobs. It works both to hold fresh oxygen and to remove the carbon dioxide the astronaut exhales. It also contains a water tank, electricity to supply the rest of the suit, and a fan to move the oxygen around.

IF AN ASTRONAUT WERE TO FLOAT AWAY FROM A SPACECRAFT, HE OR SHE COULD RELY ON A TOOL CALLED A SAFER, LOCATED IN THE BACK OF THE SUIT. THE SAFER IS MADE UP OF SMALL THRUSTER JETS WHICH COULD BE USED TO FLY BACK TO THE SHIP.

© Edwin Verin | Dreamstime.com

Spot the Difference

Spacecrafts

The Space Shuttle was a specific spacecraft that NASA operated from 1981 to 2011. The shuttle flew 135 missions, including transporting crew to build the International Space Station. The Space Shuttle is no longer used because of some limitations in the design: space travel was limited to two weeks and no farther than low Earth orbit. As scientists seek to explore deeper into space, they must create new vehicles able to withstand that journey.

Find and circle six things that are different between the two spacecrafts.

Answers on page 305

Wacky Weather

What is the difference between fog and smog?

Fog is a cloud that forms near the ground and stays low. It can occur at different times and last briefly or for a long time. Fog that forms in smoky air is called smog. Smog is often thicker than fog because smoke puts more particles in the air. Exhaust from vehicles and factories and soot from fires contribute to the smog that lies over major cities.

What is a monsoon?

A wind that reverses direction twice each year, causing two seasons, wet and dry. The heaviest rains that are part of the wet monsoon season fall in southern Asia and around the Indian Ocean.

What is a WHITEOUT?

When a blizzard's combination of low cloud cover and falling snow make it impossible to see more than a few feet or even inches ahead. People who have been caught in a whiteout say that they couldn't tell the difference between the ground and the sky!

Can hail fall in hot weather?

Yes, as long as the air high above is cold enough. Some of the biggest hailstones have fallen during summer thunderstorms, when rain droplets were frozen and refrozen in the supercooled air sweeping through high storm clouds. In fact, the largest hailstone ever recorded in the United States fell in early summer. On June 22, 2003, a hailstone measuring 18¾ inches around, and probably weighing over a pound, fell in Aurora, Nebraska.

What is the driest place on Earth?

The Atacama Desert in northern Chile. It gets almost no rainfall, except for an occasional shower only several times each century. Rain falls so seldom there that the showers average out to a mere 0.003 inches of rain a year. Now that is dry! Another very dry place is the area around the South Pole, in Antarctica. What little moisture that gathers is locked up solid—frozen into ice.

Why are some clouds white, while others are gray or black?

Because clouds are masses of water droplets and ice crystals. Sometimes shadows make clouds look gray. Usually, the denser the water within a cloud, the grayer it is—and the sooner the rain.

Looking at the Stars

ARCHAEOASTRONOMY is the study of how people in the past not only studied the sky, but the mythologies, religions, and beliefs of ancient cultures about the sky and what it might hold.

The ancient Babylonians catalogued some of the first written observations of the sky, recording dates, times, and locations of what they saw on clay tablets. Their observations were technical and mathematic, but there was also a cultural element: The observations led to the development of a calendar and a belief in constellation origins.

Modern scientists who examined the Babylonian tablets discovered that the ancient people used detailed calculations, including the connections between time, speed, and position, to determine Jupiter's path across the sky.

In ancient China, astronomers were early observers of what we now call supernovae. Back then, they called them "guest stars" and created an extensive recorded catalog of when and where they appeared, which continues to serve as a reference for modern astronomers.

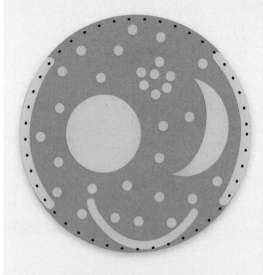

The night sky has changed a bit since humans first started recording the locations of what they saw. The motion of Earth spinning on its axis (an imaginary line through the center)—similar to a spinning top—results in a smaller circle which the axis spins along, called a precession. The full precessional motion of Earth takes 26,000 years, which means that 26,000 years ago, the sky looked exactly the same as today.

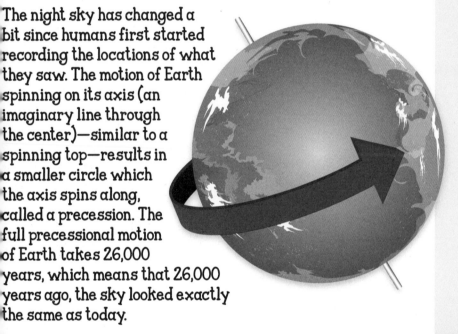

The Nebra sky disk is considered one of the oldest known illustrations of the night sky—discovered in 1999 by treasure hunters using a metal detector! This bronze disk was found in Germany and dates back to around 1600 BC. It includes images of a sun, a crescent moon, and stars, which astronomers believe are in the shape of the Pleiades star cluster.

In the modern era, there are two general types of astronomers: observational and theoretical. Theoretical astronomers spend their time thinking about how systems have evolved and changed over time, while observational astronomers do just that: observe. Their studies are direct observations of planets, galaxies, and the rest of the universe.

Across the Universe

What is the Big Bang theory?

The most widely accepted theory for how the universe began. Astronomers believe that all matter was once a single mass. Then an enormous explosion, known as the Big Bang, sent pieces flying off into space, creating galaxies, stars, and planets. The Big Bang theory says that the universe is still expanding today and that the galaxies are still moving away from each other.

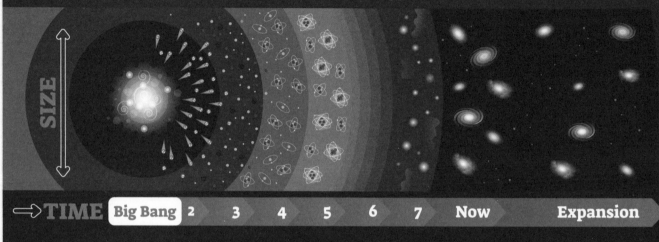

SIZE

→ TIME | Big Bang | 2 | 3 | 4 | 5 | 6 | 7 | Now | Expansion

Check Your Weight in Space!

To find out how much you would weigh on another planet, multiply your weight by the planet's force of gravity:

- Mercury 0.28
- Venus 0.85
- Earth 1.0
- Mars 0.38
- Jupiter 2.6
- Saturn 1.2
- Uranus 1.1
- Neptune 1.4

For example, a person who weighs 100 pounds on Earth would weigh 120 pounds on Saturn:

$$100 \times 1.2 = 120$$

HOW MUCH WOULD YOU WEIGH ON THE MOON?

Someone who weighs **100 pounds** on **EARTH** would weigh only **17 pounds** on the **MOON.** That is because the moon has a **LOW** force of **GRAVITY.**

On **JUPITER,** which has the **STRONGEST** gravity of all the planets, that **SAME** Earthling would weigh **260 pounds!**

WHAT IS A LIGHT-YEAR?

The distance that light travels in a year:

5,880,000,000,000 (OR ABOUT 6 TRILLION) MILES.

Scientists use light-years to describe the huge distances between objects in space.

MOST SCIENTISTS BELIEVE THAT THE UNIVERSE BEGAN ABOUT 13½ TO 14 BILLION YEARS AGO.

Do stars last forever?

No. Stars are mostly made up of hydrogen gas, which constantly burns. That's why stars shine. Eventually, they burn themselves up and explode, or simply burn out. How long that takes depends on the star. Giant stars, bigger than our sun, actually burn out quicker than smaller stars. Scientists believe our sun has been burning for 5 billion years—and it has 5 billion more to go.

WHAT IS OUR GALAXY'S BIGGEST STAR?

The Pistol Star. It is 100 times larger than our sun and it burns about 10 billion times as bright. It unleashes as much energy in 6 seconds as our sun does in one year. The Pistol Star is invisible to the naked eye because it is hidden 25,000 light-years away behind great dust clouds in the center of our Milky Way galaxy.

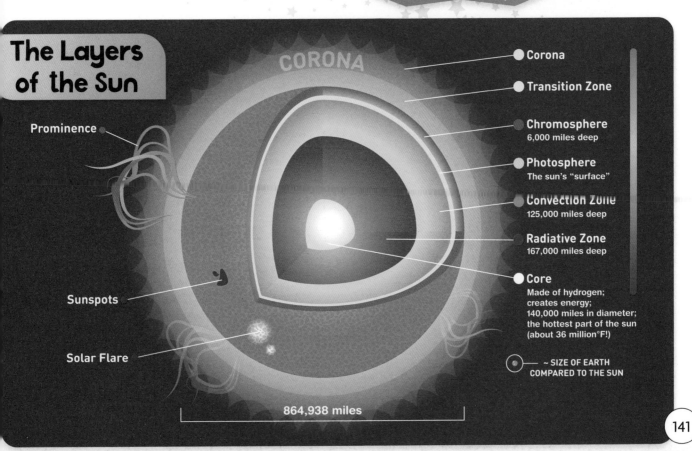

The Layers of the Sun

CORONA

Prominence

Sunspots

Solar Flare

- Corona
- Transition Zone
- Chromosphere
  6,000 miles deep
- Photosphere
  The sun's "surface"
- Convection Zone
  125,000 miles deep
- Radiative Zone
  167,000 miles deep
- Core
  Made of hydrogen; creates energy; 140,000 miles in diameter; the hottest part of the sun (about 36 million°F!)

~ SIZE OF EARTH COMPARED TO THE SUN

864,938 miles

Mars Rover, Mars Rover

Mars rovers are vehicles that explore Mars. NASA has sent four so far—*Sojourner*, *Spirit* and *Opportunity*, and *Curiosity*—and will launch a fifth in the summer of 2020.

According to NASA, there are four main goals of the explorations to Mars:

1. Discover whether there has ever been life on Mars
2. Determine the climate of Mars
3. Record and analyze the geology, or land, of Mars
4. Use the data to prepare for human exploration

Sojourner was the first Mars rover to land, in 1997. The tiniest of all the rovers—about the size of a microwave oven—*Sojourner* had to travel with a lander with airbags that would allow the rover to safely touch down on the surface. *Sojourner* took over 550 images of the landscape and gathered information about rocks, dirt, and winds. Most importantly, the research revealed that Mars was not cold and rocky, but showed evidence of once being both a wetter and warmer environment.

Rovers are important because they have wheels, so they can drive across the surface of the planet to gather samples and take pictures.

Spirit and Opportunity were twin rovers sent on the Mars Exploration Rover mission in 2003 to land on different parts of the planet, searching for data on the history of water on Mars. Spirit landed in an area with geological markings that revealed signs of past water—including places that might have been hot springs or volcanoes millions of years ago. Spirit was the first rover to take color images on another planet. In the area that Opportunity landed, there was also evidence of water: a salty ocean.

Curiosity went on a mission from 2011 to 2012 to search for conditions on Mars that would support life, examining everything from water to radiation. In 2004, scientists from around the world proposed new investigations for Curiosity to perform and tools that could be added. Eight tools were selected and added to Curiosity, including the Mars Hand Lens Imager, which snaps extreme close-up images of soil and rocks.

The Mars 2020 rover is on a mission to take the research of the four rovers that came before even further—not just to see if the planet can sustain life, but if there has ever been life on Mars. Because of this, the Mars 2020 rover has different tools, like ones that measure carbon dioxide and oxygen—which is essential information if humans are ever to visit the planet.

In the fall of 2019, students from schools across America submitted entries to name the Mars 2020 rover.

Curious About Curiosity?

The *Curiosity* rover set out on a journey to Mars on November 26, 2011, landing August 5, 2012. More than 400 scientists around the world worked on this expedition.

Curiosity's mission, according to NASA, was to answer this question: "Did Mars ever have the right environmental conditions to support small life forms called microbes?" More simply, the rover would allow scientists to search for conditions on Mars, past or present, that would be able to sustain life.

The Mars Science Laboratory built *Curiosity* to be big— around the same size as a small SUV, as tall as a basketball player, and weighing 1,982 pounds, or about as much as two horses! The rover has six wheels, each with its own motor, along with a 7-foot robotic arm. There are 10 science instruments and 17 cameras on the rover, along with other tools such as a laser and a drill.

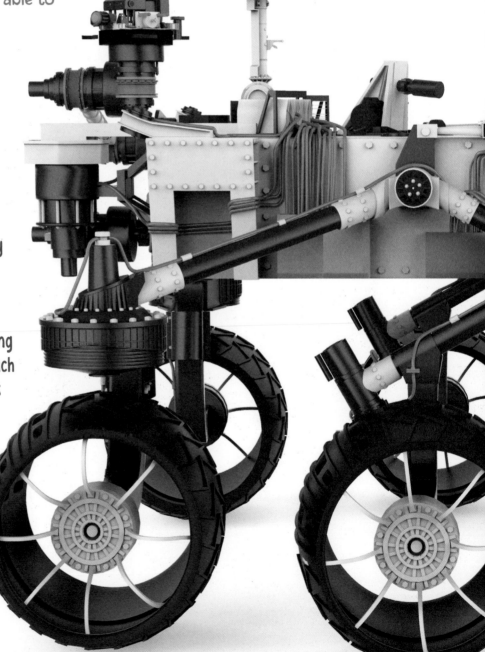

Curiosity studied the geology of Mars by drilling into rocks and gathering samples—the first of their kind. The rocks revealed that there were conditions on the planet that could support life. The samples showed minerals and geology of sustained water, which would be essential for life forms to survive on Mars.

This rover landed by deploying a parachute, then hovering above the surface using rockets, and finally touching down on its wheels and cutting itself off from the landing system.

NASA can use the data from *Curiosity* about radiation levels on Mars to help create space suits and tools for future human missions to the planet.

On the one-year anniversary of the mission in 2013, the rover sang "Happy Birthday" to itself!

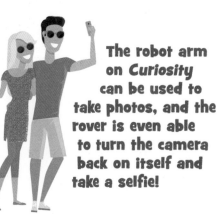

The robot arm on *Curiosity* can be used to take photos, and the rover is even able to turn the camera back on itself and take a selfie!

Fun Facts about Earth

Earth has an atmosphere that is segmented into layers.

ABOUT 70% OF EARTH'S SURFACE IS COVERED IN WATER.

ACCORDING TO SCIENTISTS, EARTH IS BETWEEN FOUR AND FIVE BILLION YEARS OLD.

Earth

The moon orbits Earth.

...th orbits the sun.

There is a great amount of life on planet Earth.

We are pretty familiar with Earth; after all, it's our home. Earth is the third planet from the sun and is just about the same size, mass, and density as Venus—but other than that, it's a unique place!

Meteors & Asteroids

A METEOR is when an ASTEROID, METEOROID, or COMET burns up when entering Earth's atmosphere at a high speed, more commonly known as a "SHOOTING STAR" when it is seen in the sky.

An ASTEROID is a rocky object, smaller than a planet but larger than a meteoroid, that orbits the sun.

A METEORITE is a meteor when it hits the ground on Earth.

A METEOROID IS BEST THOUGHT OF AS A "SPACE ROCK"—AN OBJECT IN SPACE THAT CAN RANGE IN SIZE FROM DUST TO EVEN A SMALL ASTEROID. THIS TERM ONLY APPLIES TO THESE OBJECTS IN SPACE.

When multiple meteors are visible on the same night, it is called a METEOR SHOWER. There are certain times of the year that meteor showers annually occur, caused by Earth's passing through a particular area of space with debris. The Perseids, one of the best-known meteor showers, begins mid-July and lasts for over six weeks, with peak visibility—when it's easiest to see—in the second week of August.

Word Scramble

Every year there are about 16 million thunderstorms, which means that there are around 2,000 thunderstorms happening every minute! Unscramble the letters to spell out different weather terms.

AIPRODSNR

_ _ _ _ _ _ _ _ _

GILHIGTNN

_ _ _ _ _ _ _ _ _

CDLUSO

_ _ _ _ _ _

NUEICAHRR

_ _ _ _ _ _ _ _ _

NDOOTAR

_ _ _ _ _ _ _

ALHI

_ _ _ _

UHRDENT

_ _ _ _ _ _ _

BRLZADIZ

_ _ _ _ _ _ _ _

DIWN

_ _ _ _

NWSO

_ _ _ _

Spot These Stars!

Constellations are groups of stars that appear to make shapes in the sky. Long ago, humans named these shapes after great myths and creatures. Read about these four constellations and see what they look like. Can you spot them the next time you're out stargazing?

URSA MAJOR

The name of this constellation means "great bear." The Big Dipper, a group of stars familiar to many, is a small part of Ursa Major. The best time to see this bear is during spring, though it is visible all year. The handle of the Big Dipper is the bear's tail. Once you spot the dipper, trace a line north connecting the two stars on the far outer edge of the bowl to find Polaris, the North Star.

URSA MINOR

A companion to the "great bear," this "little bear" also contains the Little Dipper. Once you spot Ursa Major, use it to find Polaris, or the North Star. That will lead you directly to the Little Dipper: Polaris makes up the star on the end of the handle.

TAURUS

Best spotted in late October and early November, Taurus is named for a white bull in Greek mythology. Located northwest of Orion, this constellation also contains the Pleiades cluster of stars. While only the brightest ones can be spotted without a telescope, the Pleiades, nicknamed the "Seven Sisters," are a group of many hot, blue stars that have formed within the last 100 million years.

ORION

Named for a giant hunter in Greek mythology, Orion is one of the easiest constellations to spot, visible from almost anywhere on Earth—though it is brightest in the winter sky in the Northern Hemisphere. To spot Orion, look for his belt: three bright stars, named Mintaka, Alnilam, and Alnitak, in equal distance from one another. The belt will lead you to two bright stars above and two below which form his shoulders and legs.

THE POSITIONS OF STARS MOVE VERY SLOWLY, ESPECIALLY IN THE PERIOD OF A HUMAN LIFETIME. STARS ARE ALWAYS MOVING, SO CONSTELLATIONS DO CHANGE—BUT ONLY SLIGHTLY. THE PATTERNS WILL CHANGE COMPLETELY OVER TENS OF THOUSANDS OF YEARS.

Windy Day

What is wind?

Do you sometimes feel like the air is moving on a windy day? Well, it is! Wind is just another name for moving air. Air moves all around our planet. It can be a gentle breeze or a forceful gust. Gentle winds can fly a kite and make wind chimes sing, while strong winds can tear down trees and cause major destruction.

HOW IS THE WIND MEASURED?

The Beaufort scale is a scientific measurement for the intensity of weather based on wind power. It was developed by the British naval commander Sir Francis Beaufort around 1806. The scale goes from 0 to 12, ranging from calm to hurricane force winds.

Where is Tornado Alley?

In the Central and Southern plains states between the Rocky Mountains and the Appalachian Mountains. The United States has about 1,000 tornadoes each year, and most of them occur in Tornado Alley. More tornadoes strike Tornado Alley than any other place in the world. The world's deadliest tornado—the Tri-State Tornado of March 18, 1925—cut a path 219 miles long across Missouri, Illinois, and Indiana. It killed 695 people, injured 1,980, and left 11,000 homeless.

What makes wind blow?

Temperature changes. The sun heats whatever it touches, and when it heats up air, the air becomes warmer and lighter. As warm air rises, it's replaced by cool air, which is made up of gases that move slower and are closer together. Then this air warms, too. This constant movement of air rising and being replaced creates wind.

WHAT IS A DUST DEVIL?

Dust devils are whirlwinds caused by intense heating of dry ground, usually in desert areas. A rapid updraft of warm air starts a spin that can carry dust half a mile into the sky.

Do hurricanes always spin in the same direction?

That depends on where you are. In the northern hemisphere, hurricanes spin in a counterclockwise direction. In the southern hemisphere, the same type of storm, called a cyclone, spins clockwise. That is the Coriolis force at work. It is caused by the rotation of Earth, which forces things moving freely across Earth's surface to move on a curved path—including wind and ocean currents.

Electricity, Lightning, and Thunder

WHAT CAUSES LIGHTNING?

The rapid movement of ice crystals in storm clouds builds up electric charges (similar to the charge that builds up when you rub a balloon on your sleeve). Electric charges also form on the ground beneath the clouds. When a negative charge meets a positive charge, look out! A huge electrical current—a lightning bolt—shoots between the two charges. Most lightning bolts stay up in the clouds; only about a quarter of them strike the ground.

WHAT IS THUNDER?

Lightning heats the air along its path to temperatures as high as 54,000°F! As it heats and then cools, this air expands and contracts, forming a series of shock waves that travel at the speed of sound. Our ears pick up those fast-moving waves as the boom, crash, and rumble of thunder.

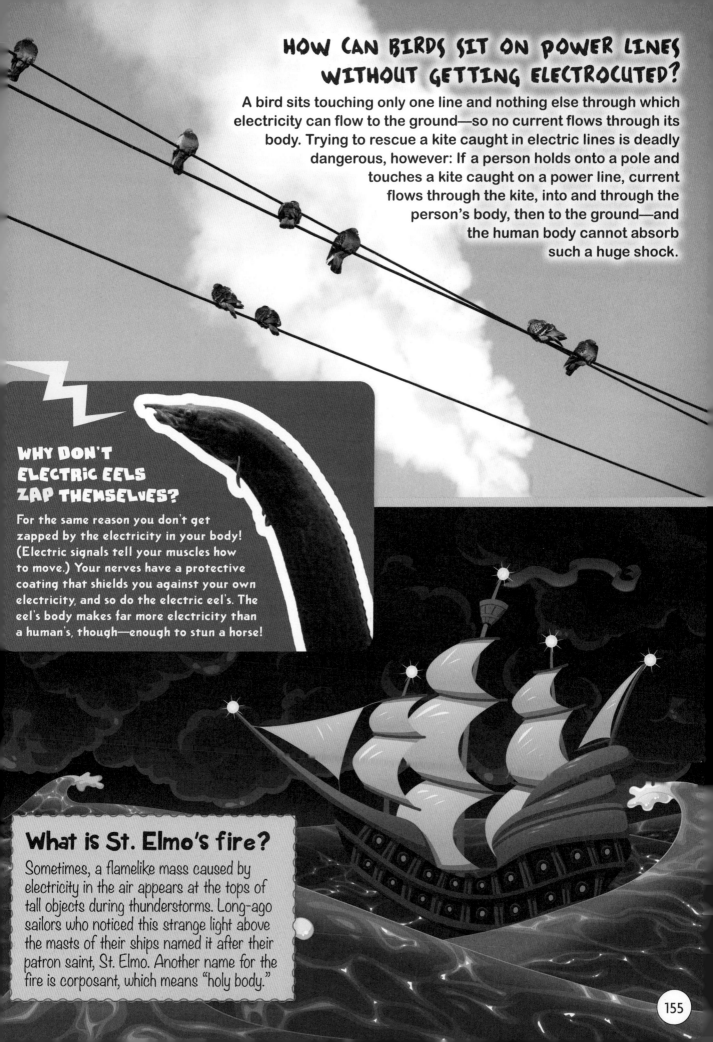

HOW CAN BIRDS SIT ON POWER LINES WITHOUT GETTING ELECTROCUTED?

A bird sits touching only one line and nothing else through which electricity can flow to the ground—so no current flows through its body. Trying to rescue a kite caught in electric lines is deadly dangerous, however: If a person holds onto a pole and touches a kite caught on a power line, current flows through the kite, into and through the person's body, then to the ground—and the human body cannot absorb such a huge shock.

WHY DON'T ELECTRIC EELS ZAP THEMSELVES?

For the same reason you don't get zapped by the electricity in your body! (Electric signals tell your muscles how to move.) Your nerves have a protective coating that shields you against your own electricity, and so do the electric eel's. The eel's body makes far more electricity than a human's, though—enough to stun a horse!

What is St. Elmo's fire?

Sometimes, a flamelike mass caused by electricity in the air appears at the tops of tall objects during thunderstorms. Long-ago sailors who noticed this strange light above the masts of their ships named it after their patron saint, St. Elmo. Another name for the fire is corposant, which means "holy body."

155

Down to Earth

What's the star nearest to Earth?

Don't wait until dark to find it. Don't even take out your telescope.
It's our very own daytime star, the sun, just 93 million miles away.
The next closest star is Proxima Centauri, and it's 25 trillion miles from Earth.

WHAT IS THE OZONE LAYER?

It's part of Earth's atmosphere. As you go up from the ground, the gases that make up the atmosphere change. These "layers" of gas have different names. The ozone layer is about 12 to 30 miles above Earth's surface. Ozone is a form of oxygen that absorbs much of the sun's ultraviolet radiation and prevents it from reaching the ground. If this radiation did reach ground level, it would be harmful to most forms of life.

How big is Earth?

Huge! If we broke Earth into pieces and hauled it away at a rate of 20 tons per second, it would take

1,000,000,000,000,000,000

(that's one quintillion!) years to get rid of the whole planet.

How can you be moving, even when standing still?

Not only is Earth spinning on its axis at about 1,083 miles per hour, it is also zooming around the sun at more than 65,000 miles per hour. The crustal plate beneath your feet is moving, too—very, very slowly.

How did land develop?

Land was created from volcanic activity. Lava cooled after eruptions to form the first layers of foundation.

Spinosaurus

If you thought *T. rex* was the biggest dinosaur ever, meet *Spinosaurus*! This dinosaur holds the record as the largest meat-eating dinosaur of them all. Paleontologists believe this dinosaur also speared fish out of water for a meal. *Spinosaurus* lived during the same time period as *Sarcosuchus*, the "Super Croc," so these two creatures may have fought each other to catch fish.

SPINOSAURUS'S TEETH WERE ABOUT 5 INCHES LONG.

WITH ITS **LONG, THIN HEAD** AND RELATIVELY SHORT, **SHARP TEETH**, THIS DINOSAUR LOOKED SIMILAR TO A **CROCODILE**.

SPINOSAURUS MAINLY WALKED UPRIGHT ON ITS TWO BACK LEGS, BUT IT MAY HAVE OCCASIONALLY WALKED ON ALL FOURS.

DID YOU KNOW?

The name *Spinosaurus* means "spine lizard."

Spinosaurus had to adjust its diet according to the season.

THE SAIL ON *SPINOSAURUS'S* BACK MAY HAVE BEEN USED TO CONTROL BODY TEMPERATURE, OR IT MAY HAVE BEEN USED TO MAKE THE DINOSAUR LOOK EVEN **BIGGER** THAN IT WAS.

The Zodiac

More than 3,000 years ago, the Babylonians created the zodiac, dividing the year into 12 equal parts with each part assigned a constellation. According to ancient Babylonian stories, however, there were originally 13 constellations—but that number didn't divide up neatly, so they cut one out!

Astronomy and astrology may sound similar, but they are not the same. Astronomy is the scientific study of space, the physical universe, and celestial phenomena. Astrology is a belief that the position of the stars can reveal information about human life events, personalities, and traits— better known as horoscopes.

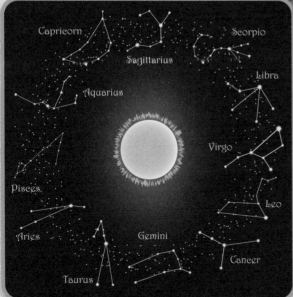

The constellations known as the zodiac are the ones that move along the same path the sun takes every year, known as the ecliptic. Astrologists use these signs of the zodiac in their projections, but they are based on astronomers' research of how these constellations mark the passing of a year on Earth.

Crack the Code

National Park Pride

Solve the cryptogram below to reveal a famous quote from John Muir. Use the key below to fill in the blanks and reveal the quote.

1=S	5=F	9=H	13=R	17=V	21=O	25=M
2=D	6=K	10=B	14=I	18=C	22=G	26=Z
3=U	7=Q	11=N	15=A	19=L	23=Y	
4=E	8=P	12=W	16=T	20=X	24=J	

"
16 9 4   25 21 3 11 16 15 14 11 1

15 13 4   18 15 19 19 14 11 22

15 11 2   14   25 3 1 16   22 21."

Considered by many in the United States as the "Father of our National Parks," John Muir was an early naturalist and conservationist. He founded the Sierra Club, a California wildlife conservation organization, and his writings to the US government contributed to the protection of many natural areas: the Grand Canyon, Sequoia National Park, Mount Rainier, and Yosemite.

Answers on page 307

Danger Zone

What is hazmat?

"Hazmat" is short for "hazardous material." Hazmats are waste products created during the manufacture of many modern products, such as toys, clothes, computers, and cars. Some household items—such as old paint cans, batteries, and weed killers—are also considered hazmats.

HAZARDOUS

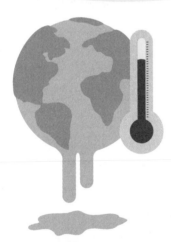

WHAT IS GLOBAL WARMING?

Scientists worry that we are making Earth too warm by adding to the greenhouse effect. Cars, power plants, and other human-made devices give off much more carbon dioxide gas (CO_2) than would naturally occur, which traps more of the sun's heat in Earth's atmosphere. The problem gets worse when large areas of forest are cut down for timber or to clear land for farming. Live trees absorb CO_2 and give off oxygen, which most living things need in order to survive.

What is the greenhouse effect?

The glass of a greenhouse traps the sun's heat inside. Earth is surrounded by its atmosphere—layers of gases that protect it from extreme heat or cold. Earth's atmosphere acts like glass, keeping the planet's surface warmer than it would be otherwise. If it didn't, Earth would be covered with ice.

greenhouse gases

Is there pollution in space?

Yes. Traveling in space requires a lot of equipment. Space shuttles and satellites leave rocket boosters, empty fuel tanks, nuts, bolts, and paint chips in their wake. It can take many years for this space junk to hit Earth's atmosphere, where it will burn up. Each year, dozens of rockets are launched, which means that a lot of junk is left floating around.

Does radiation cause problems—or solve them?

Both. Radioactive waste products from nuclear power plants are a problem: If not disposed of carefully, they harm living things. Such waste can be sealed in special containers and buried or stored safely. Even so, many people fear that the radioactive waste might leak out and contaminate air, water, or soil. However, radiation can also be helpful. For instance, doctors often use radioactive materials to kill cancer cells in patients.

Do buildings ever get sick?

Yes. A building may be suspected of having sick building syndrome (SBS) when many people living or working in it start feeling ill at the same time. Symptoms may include headaches; irritation of the eyes, nose, and throat; nausea; and fatigue. Buildings with SBS usually have poor air circulation. Even worse, irritating chemicals may have become trapped in the air supply. To heal the building, experts must find and correct the problem.

Fun Facts
about the Moon

THE MOON IS ABOUT 250,000 MILES FROM EARTH.

THE MOON IS **4 1/2 BILLION** YEARS OLD.

THE MOON REFLECTS LIGHT FROM THE SUN.

How does the moon affect Earth?
The moon's gravity creates tides. As Earth rotates, different parts face the moon. When the moon passes water, the water is attracted to its gravitational pull. Surfers, sailors, and beach lovers are affected by the moon!

Moon

There is no atmosphere, wind, or weather on the moon.

Although it appears to change shape, the moon is actually just revolving around Earth, altering its exposure to the sun.

WATER was discovered on the moon in 2009.

THERE ARE CRATERS, LAVA PLAINS, VALLEYS, AND MOUNTAINS ON THE MOON'S SURFACE. ASTRONOMERS BELIEVE CRATERS APPEARED BILLIONS OF YEARS AGO AFTER METEORS STRUCK THE MOON.

THE MAN IN THE MOON

Some people are certain they've seen a man's face in the moon. Others think there appears to be some sort of animal in the moon. The images they see are created by shadows cast from the moon's mountains and craters. When you observe the moon early or late in the month, more shadows will appear on its surface because the light it reflects from the sun will be less bright.

Apatosaurus

The *Apatosaurus,* once known as the *Brontosaurus,* had a very, very long neck! This dinosaur was a sauropod—this means it had a long neck and tail, and it walked on all four legs. Paleontologists are still not sure about its posture.

THE *APATOSAURUS* IS THOUGHT TO HAVE BEEN ONE OF THE LARGEST LAND ANIMALS EVER TO HAVE ROAMED THE EARTH. IT WEIGHED ABOUT THE SAME AS AN 18-WHEELER!

The spikes on the thumbs were up to 6 inches long.

SCIENTISTS THINK IT ONLY TOOK ABOUT **10 YEARS** FOR **APATOSAURUS** TO REACH ITS **FULL SIZE.**

The small babies, or "hatchlings," of Apatosaurus might have been light enough to **run** on two feet.

Brrrrrr

How cold does it get in Antarctica?

The lowest temperature ever recorded anywhere on Earth was -128.6°F at Russia's Vostok research station at the South Pole, on July 21, 1983.

What is the absolute coldest temperature?

Absolute zero, or -459.67°F. Scientists have been able to get within two millionths of a degree of this point in labs. Nothing moves at this temperature, not even a molecule!

Where is it colder, the North Pole or the South Pole?

The South Pole. It sits on a mountain, where it is colder than at sea level. The North Pole is located on an ice cap floating on the Arctic Ocean. Warmth from the ocean keeps the North Pole's temperature higher than it would be otherwise.

WHY DOES ICE FLOAT?

Substances are usually most dense when they are solid because that is when their molecules are most compact—but water is different. Water molecules are farther apart when water is solid (ice) than when it is liquid. This means that ice is less dense than water—so it floats!

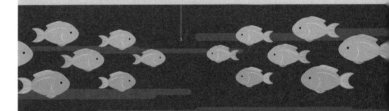

Do lakes freeze in cold weather?

Only on the surface. When water cools, its molecules slow down and get closer together, causing it to become more dense and to sink. Once water gets colder than 39°F (4°C), however, the molecules start to expand, and water becomes lighter and rises. Because of this, the coldest water freezes into a layer of ice that floats on the surface.

What is permafrost, and how can it cause problems?

Permafrost is soil that stays frozen even in summer. It is found in places close to the poles, such as Alaska and Siberia. Permafrost can cause problems for buildings constructed on it. Warmth can leak through the building's foundation, melting the permafrost, which softens the soil—making it soft enough for the building to sink!

169

Fun Facts
about Mars

The atmosphere on Mars is very weak and thin.

Is there life on Mars? You've always heard stories about aliens from Mars. Are they true? So far, NASA has not found any evidence of life in any form on Mars.

While scientists have yet to discover water in its liquid form on Mars, it does appear as a solid and vapor.

The surface of Mars is covered in a fine dust that is rich in iron oxide—rust! This is why the planet appears red.

Mars is a cold planet. The average temperature is -22°F during the day and -148°F at night.

Mars

Mars is the closet planet to Earth. We have sent more space probes to Mars than to any other planet, so we know it the best. (See pages 142-145 about the Mars rovers.)

Although we sometimes think Mars is similar to Earth in size, its diameter is half the size of Earth's, and it has an even smaller mass.

Like Earth, Mars is tilted on its axis. This causes it to have two seasons: summer and winter. The seasons on Mars are longer, because Mars's distance to the sun changes throughout its elliptical orbit.

Mars has craters, polar ice caps, volcanoes, canyons, plains, and channels.

Mars is home to the tallest and largest known volcano in the solar system, Mons Olympus, but it is extinct. Scientists do not believe that any volcanoes on Mars are currently active.

Mars has a system of canyons called the Valles Marineris that are 10 times as long as the Grand Canyon.

Dinosaurs

Where and when was the first complete dinosaur skeleton assembled and displayed?

Hadrosaurus foulkii was unearthed in New Jersey in 1858. It was the first skeleton found with enough bones to show what dinosaurs looked like. Ten years later, a mounted specimen was created from those bones and displayed at the Academy of Natural Science in Philadelphia. (The photo above shows a model of a skeleton at a dinosaur park in Belgorod, Russia.)

WHICH DINOSAUR COULD BE CALLED A LIVING TANK?

Ankylosaurus was a herbivore that was sometimes called a living tank because the top of its body was covered with thick armor made of bone.

WHICH DINOSAUR WAS MOST LIKELY TO FLUNK A TEST?

Scientists estimate a dinosaur's intelligence by comparing its brain size to its body size. Sauropods, such as *Diplodocus*, could be considered the least intelligent, because they had the smallest brains in relation to their large body size. *Troodon*—which had a large brain in relation to its small body size—may have been one of the smartest.

WHERE DID DINOSAURS LEAVE THE TINIEST FOSSIL FOOTPRINTS?

The smallest known dinosaur footprints are in Nova Scotia, Canada. The inch-long tracks were made by a baby meat-eating dinosaur that was such a peewee, it would have hid in your hands.

Which animal laid the largest eggs?

No, it wasn't a 100-foot long dinosaur. The largest dinosaur eggs ever found are the size of cantaloupes. However, the moa—an extinct bird of New Zealand—laid eggs as big as watermelons!

Food Chains

A food chain represents the transfer of energy from one species to another. It shows how each living thing gets food and how nutrients and energy are passed along. A food chain begins with plant life and ends with animal life.

All living things need energy to grow. Some living things make energy into a usable form from sunlight, water, and air. They are the producers. Some living things use this energy. They are the consumers.

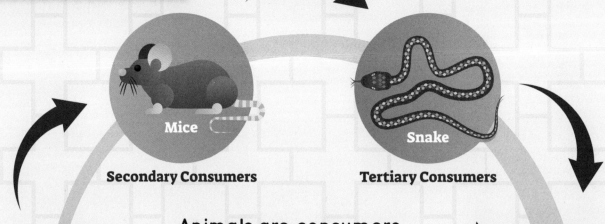

Mice

Secondary Consumers

Snake

Tertiary Consumers

Animals are consumers. Some animals eat plants, some animals eat other animals, and still others eat both—but all animals need energy to live and grow, and they get most of their energy from what they eat.

Grasshopper

Primary Consumer

Hawk

Final Consumers

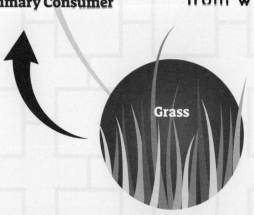

Grass

Producer

Fungi

Decomposers

1. Green plants are producers of energy. They make their own food using sunlight, water, air, soil, and other elements.

2. A primary consumer is an animal that eats producers.

3. Secondary, tertiary, and final consumers all eat other consumers, and some also eat producers.

4. When an animal dies, decomposers such as fungi (like mushrooms) and bacteria break down the animal and turn it into nutrients for the soil. These nutrients are used again by plants. Then the energy chain begins again.

HERE ARE FOUR DIFFERENT TYPES OF CONSUMERS IN THE ANIMAL KINGDOM.

CARNIVORE

This is an animal that only eats other animals.

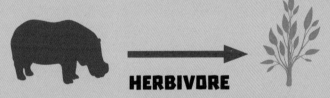

HERBIVORE

This is an animal that only eats plants.

OMNIVORE

This is an animal that eats both plants and animals.

SCAVENGER

This is an animal that eats dead animals.

Hard Stuff

WHAT IS PETRIFIED WOOD?

A fossil. Over thousands of years, water seeping through buried wood slowly replaces parts of the plant with minerals, such as silica and calcium carbonate. This makes the wood look as if it has petrified, or turned to stone. Sometimes this mineralization is so thorough that the ancient wood is preserved with all of its original details intact. The famous Petrified Forest, located in northeastern Arizona, contains fossilized trees 225 million years old.

Will fool's gold make you rich?

No way. Fool's gold is pyrite, a mineral that contains iron and sulfur. Prospectors were often fooled into thinking that pyrite was gold because it looks metallic and has a golden color. That is how it got its nickname! Geologists never mistake the two. Gold, one of the heaviest metals, can be pounded into other shapes, stretched into wire, and cut into slices. Pyrite has none of these properties.

Amber is fossilized sap, or resin, from trees that lived about 40 to 60 million years ago. Sometimes the transparent yellow pieces of amber contain insects, leaves, or parts of other living things that were trapped in the sticky sap before it hardened.

WHAT IS SO INTERESTING ABOUT THE LA BREA TAR PITS?

Their record of prehistoric life. Between 10,000 and 40,000 years ago, many animals became trapped in the pools of sticky tar that oozed from below Earth's surface. Bones of saber-toothed tigers, mammoths, horses, and camels have all been found here, along with plant fossils. This ancient site is in the midst of a modern city—Los Angeles, California.

HOW WAS COAL FORMED?

Hundreds of millions of years ago, trees and other plants died in ancient swamps and sank into the water, layer upon layer.

As the swamplands sank, seas covered them, laying silt and sand, called sediment, over the decaying plants. As layers of sediment built up, pressure on the plant material increased, forcing out the water and pressing together what was left.

Over time, this changed the plant matter into coal.

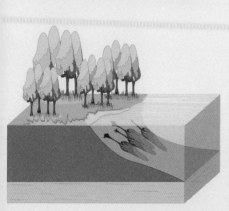

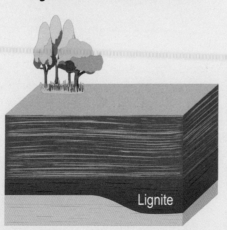

Lignite

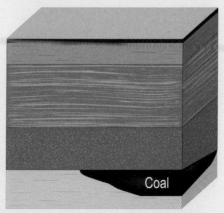

Coal

Millions of years

Continental Drift

About 150 million years ago, all of today's continents were joined together in one supercontinent called Pangaea (pan-JEE-uh), but the seafloor spread slowly, pushing them apart.

Pangaea
(250 million years ago)

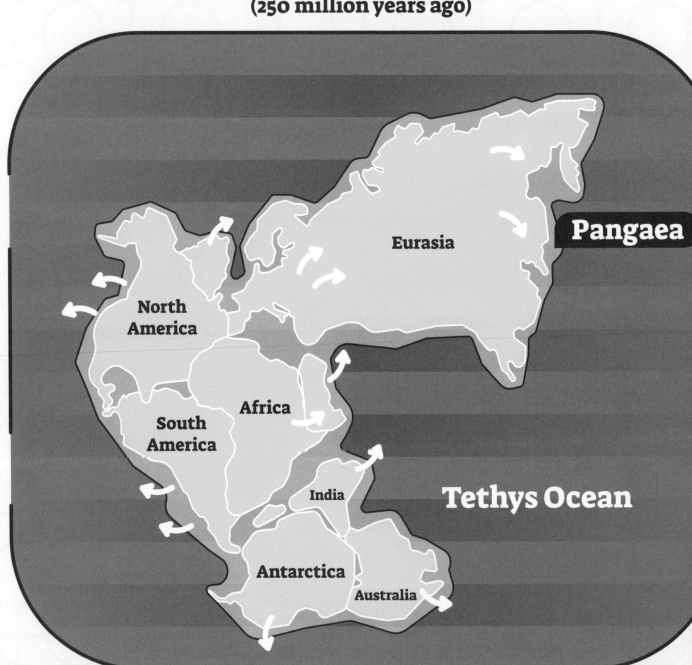

Laurasia and Gondwana
(200 million years ago)

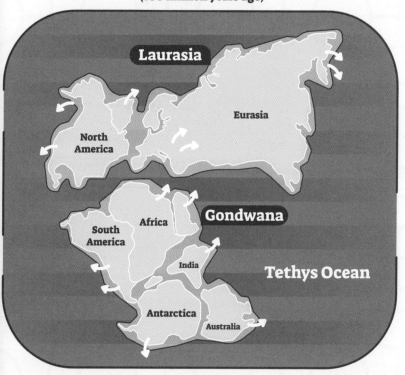

Laurasia

Eurasia

North America

Gondwana

South America

Africa

India

Antarctica

Australia

Tethys Ocean

The continents are constantly moving—very, very slowly. Sections of Earth's crust, called tectonic plates, shift over time.

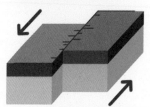

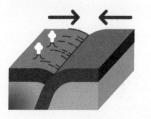

Today, Earth's eight large plates are still moving apart, at the rate of about 2 to 4 inches a year.

Present

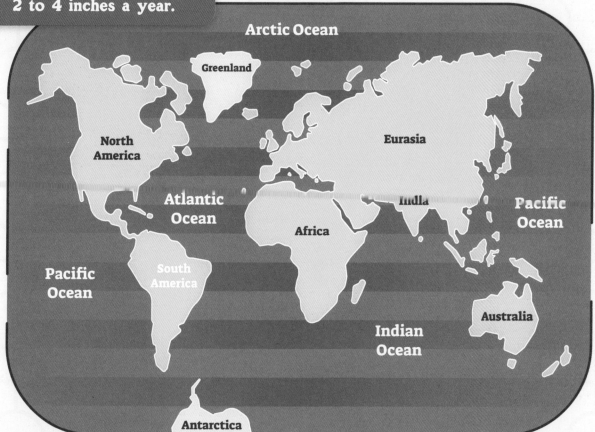

Arctic Ocean

Greenland

North America

Eurasia

Atlantic Ocean

India

Pacific Ocean

Africa

Pacific Ocean

South America

Indian Ocean

Australia

Antarctica

Mind-Blowing Facts about the Universe

According to data from the Hubble Space Telescope, the universe used to expand slower than it does today: the rate of expansion is accelerating. The scientists who discovered this in 1998 won the Nobel Prize in Physics.

There are still many unanswered questions about the universe, its size, and whether it is the only universe that exists. According to some scientists, the universe could be around 93 billion light-years in diameter—but there's no proof that the universe even has an end, or limit, at all.

There is no sound in empty space: Space does not have air, so sound, or vibrations in the air, cannot exist.

Scientists believe the universe is expanding faster because of dark energy—a mysterious, unexplainable force that cannot be seen, which is pulling apart the cosmos at faster speeds.

The galaxies in the universe vary in shape, including oval-like shapes or shapes like toothpicks or rings, but about two-thirds of the galaxies so far discovered are spiral-shaped like our Milky Way.

DID YOU KNOW?

Scientists believe there could be as many as **100 billion galaxies** in the universe.

Making Words

Aquatic Wordsmith

There are many different types of bodies of water. Here are just a few: A **SPRING** is water that flows from underground up to the surface; a **CREEK** is a small stream; a **BAYOU** is slow-moving water with marshy vegetation, or plants; a **TRIBUTARY** is a stream that flows into a larger stream or river; and a **MEANDER** is a bend in a winding river.

Look at the word below. How many words, of three or more letters, can you make using only the letters in **MEANDER**? Fill out your answers on the lines below.

MEANDER

Unusual Items Brought to Space

Astronauts on the *Discovery* space shuttle brought actor Mark Hamill's original prop lightsaber from his role as Luke Skywalker in the 1977 film *Star Wars* on their journey to space in 2007—the film's 30th anniversary.

The Jamestown Settlement was the original colony English settlers established in 1607 in what would later become the United States. About 400 years later, in 2007, a cargo tag with the name of the settlement, the only one of its kind, was taken into space aboard the *Atlantis* shuttle.

In 1985, the first dinosaur went to space. Astronaut Loren Acton brought with him bone and eggshell fragments from the *Maiasaura peeblesorum*, a hadrosaur, to SpaceLab 2. Then in 1998, the shuttle *Endeavor* brought with it the skull of a *Coelophysis*, a small theropod, borrowed from the Carnegie Museum of History.

Astronaut Thomas Pesquet hoped to bring his saxophone with him to the International Space Station, but he was unable to bring the instrument. As a birthday surprise, NASA sent the saxophone with a cargo flight, and his crew members gave him the instrument on his 39th birthday.

Amelia Earhart's acclaimed transatlantic flights, the first of their kind for a female pilot, made her a hero to many—especially women pilots and astronauts. To honor her trailblazing achievement 82 years later, astronaut Shannon Walker brought Earhart's watch to the International Space Station: the very watch Earhart wore during her two transatlantic flights.

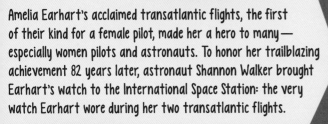

Pizza delivery!

In 2001, Pizza Hut became the first outer-space pizza place when they used a rocket to deliver a pizza to the Russian cosmonauts at the International Space Station. Pizza Hut added lots of extra seasoning, as human taste buds are dulled in space.

Buzz Lightyear finally traveled to "infinity and beyond" in 2008, when he spent 15 months in the International Space Station. A 12-inch action figure of this beloved *Toy Story* character was used to help teach kids about gravity and space life—even leaving the shuttle with an astronaut to help demonstrate those concepts out in open space.

Sky Above

WHY IS THE SKY BLUE?

Molecules and dust particles in Earth's atmosphere scatter sunlight. Short light waves, such as violet and blue, scatter better than long red and orange light waves. The blue color that we see is a mix of blue, violet, green, and tiny amounts of other colors scattered across the sky. If you were standing on the moon, which does not have an atmosphere to catch and scatter light, the sky would look black.

Do sun dogs bark?

No. Sun dogs are bright spots of light appearing on one or both sides of the sun. They are caused by sunlight passing through ice crystals in the air.

What are the northern lights?

Shimmering, brightly colored bands of light that appear in the night sky near the North Magnetic Pole. They are caused by particles streaming from the sun, which make gases in Earth's upper atmosphere glow. The best places to see the northern lights—also called the aurora borealis—are northern Alaska, Canada's Hudson Bay, northern Norway, and northern Siberia. Southern lights—called the aurora australis—can be seen near the South Magnetic Pole.

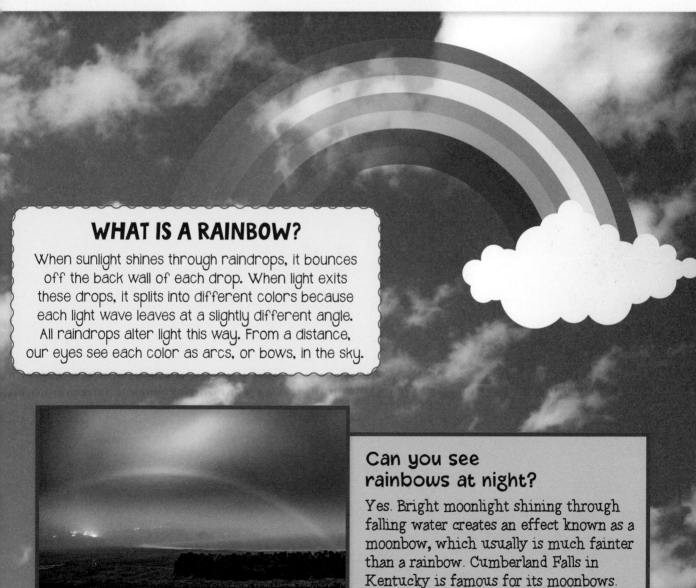

WHAT IS A RAINBOW?

When sunlight shines through raindrops, it bounces off the back wall of each drop. When light exits these drops, it splits into different colors because each light wave leaves at a slightly different angle. All raindrops alter light this way. From a distance, our eyes see each color as arcs, or bows, in the sky.

Can you see rainbows at night?

Yes. Bright moonlight shining through falling water creates an effect known as a moonbow, which usually is much fainter than a rainbow. Cumberland Falls in Kentucky is famous for its moonbows.

Monkey Business

Monkeys and apes are primates, but they differ from each other in many ways. Monkeys have tails, and apes do not. Monkeys are usually smaller and do not stand as upright as apes. A monkey's brain is a bit smaller, and monkeys have more of a snout than apes.

THERE ARE **264** KNOWN MONKEY SPECIES.

The smallest monkeys, like this pygmy marmoset, are about 6 inches long and weigh only 4 ounces.

THE **LARGEST** monkeys, LIKE THIS MANDRILL, CAN BE UP TO **3 FEET LONG** AND WEIGH UP TO **77 POUNDS.**

Most monkeys have long, powerful tails. They use them for balance, leaping, and even holding onto branches!

Many types of monkeys live high up in the trees all the time. They are called arboreal. Others go back and forth between land and trees.

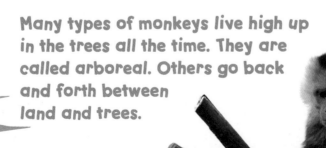

Endangered Animals

Did you know these mammals are in danger of becoming extinct?

West Indian Manatees
A manatee is a huge but gentle creature, considered to be one of the most endangered marine mammals. They have no natural enemies, but collisions with boats kill manatees every year.

North Atlantic Right Whales
This species is endangered due to entanglement with commercial ocean fishing gear and ship strikes.

© Sergei Nezhinskii | Dreamstime.com

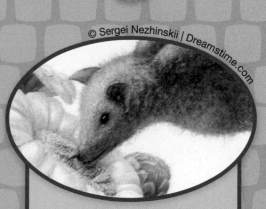

GRAY WOLVES
Scientists believe that wolves are intelligent, social creatures who rarely harm humans. Destruction of their habitats is leading to the gray wolves' extinction.

LONG-NOSED BATS
Bats play an important role in nature. They eat insects and pests, pollinate plants, and spread seeds. Long-nosed bats that live in the southwestern United States and Mexico are threatened due to habitat destruction and killings by humans.

FLORIDA PANTHERS
These members of the cat family are in big trouble! They have lost their homes due to human activity such as land development. That leads to habitat fragmentation, which means they can't easily move from one part of their habitat to another.

Fun Facts about Jupiter

Jupiter is a great distance from the sun, yet it is a hot planet.

JUPITER IS **HUGE!** IT'S **LARGER** THAN **ALL** THE OTHER **PLANETS** AND THEIR **MOONS** COMBINED. IT MEASURES ABOUT **88,700 MILES** AROUND ITS EQUATOR.

What is the Great Red Spot?

It is a huge red, oval spot south of Jupiter's equator that is actually a large storm, kind of like a hurricane. The spot has been around for nearly three centuries, but astronomers think it may vanish one day. In 2006, a new small red spot appeared as three smaller spots collided and turned red!

Jupiter

Jupiter is known as a
GAS GIANT
since most of its enormous size comes from many layers of gas that surround its core.

Jupiter has rings, which were probably formed from material ejected from Jupiter's moons when they were struck by meteors.

WHAT CAUSES JUPITER'S DIFFERENT COLORS?

Jupiter's primary gases, hydrogen and helium, do not have color. The chemicals within these gases—methane, ammonia, phosphine, and others—are responsible. You can find cream, yellow, pink, orange, brown, and red among the planet's different colors.

How many known satellites, or moons, does Jupiter have?

There are 50 total—but even more temporary ones that have yet to be confirmed and named. Jupiter's largest moons are named Ganymede, Europa, Io, and Callisto.

WHAT ARE THE MOONS OF JUPITER LIKE?

Ganymede is made mostly of ice and rock with large areas of ridges and valleys. Europa is about the same size as Earth's moon. It has a surface of ice with low ridges. Io is the closest moon to Jupiter, and it has many active volcanoes. Instead of releasing lava, these volcanoes spew sulfur compounds. Callisto is the farthest moon from Jupiter with shallow craters.

WHAT ARE THE OTHER GAS GIANTS?

Saturn, Uranus, and Neptune. The gas giants are the biggest planets in the solar system, with small rocky cores, semisolid mantles—and large outer layers of gases, of course. Each gas giant is circled by rings.

189

Allosaurus

Look out! It's an *Allosaurus*! One of the first well-known dinosaurs, this meat-eating giant had very sharp claws that it may have used to catch prey. When smaller dinosaurs saw *Allosaurus,* they ran for their lives! This terrifying dinosaur was a frightening predator.

Allosaurus had a jaw full of very sharp teeth, shaped like mini saws. *Allosaurus* constantly shed and grew new teeth.

Some teeth measured 3 to 4 inches in length.

DID YOU KNOW?

Allosaurus used its long tail for balance.

The name *Allosaurus* means "different lizard."

Found in 1991, "Big Al" is the name of the most famous *Allosaurus* SKELETON.

Animal Facts

Which is smaller, a motmot or a mola?

Definitely a motmot. The motmot is a long-tailed bird found in the forests of Central and South America. The largest motmots are only about 20 inches long. The mola, also called the ocean sunfish, is much larger. It can weigh 4,000 pounds and be 11 feet long!

How can the toucan fly with such a big bill?

The toucan's bill is large, but it is filled with air pockets, so it doesn't weigh much. Bright colors help the birds blend in among bright jungle colors. Thanks to its huge bill, a toucan can stand securely on a strong branch, reach for a piece of fruit, tilt its head, and gobble up its snack whole!

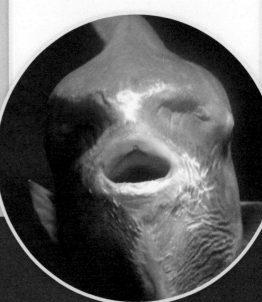

Why does a baby kangaroo depend on its mother's pouch?

A baby kangaroo, called a joey, is blind and helpless at birth—and weighs only a little more than a thumbtack. The joey crawls into its mother's pouch, where it finds warmth and food. It does not leave the pouch for about six months.

Why don't birds fall off their perches when they sleep?

Leg locks. A bird bends its legs to perch. Bending the legs automatically pulls on muscles that make the bird's toes contract around its perch, holding the bird in place.

What are the hyrax's closest relatives?

You would never guess it by looking at one, but the hyrax is related to elephants and dugongs (manatee-like sea mammals). The hyrax is a furry, rodentlike animal about the size of a rabbit. Hyraxes live in Africa and the Middle East.

WHAT IS AN ANTLION?

The larva of a dragonfly-like insect, also known as a doodlebug. The antlion digs a cone-shaped pit into loose soil or sand, then hides at the bottom and waits for small insects to fall into the pit. While the insects struggle to climb up the steep, slippery sides of the pit to escape, the antlion snaps them up in its big jaws.

Sound Travel

Sounds are made when something vibrates back and forth.

Sound waves travel to our ears and vibrate our eardrums, helping us hear.

VOLUME describes if a sound is soft or loud. Louder volumes travel greater distances than softer volumes. They have more energy.

SOUND TRAVELS SLOWER THAN LIGHT. THIS IS WHY YOU WILL SEE A FLASH OF LIGHTNING BEFORE YOU HEAR THE CRACK OF THUNDER; BOTH HAPPEN AT THE SAME TIME, BUT LIGHT REACHES US BEFORE SOUND DOES.

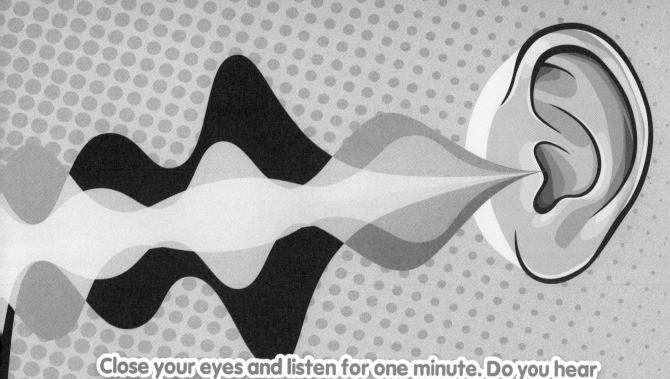

Close your eyes and listen for one minute. Do you hear anything? In just 60 seconds, you can hear many different sounds from far and near. Sound depends on vibration or movement, high or low pitches, and frequency.

Try to experiment with sound. Listen to different sounds in your neighborhood—dogs barking, cars moving, birds singing. It may sound like a whole new world once you understand some facts about sound.

Look at the picture to see how sound from the fire truck's siren travels, warning people to leave the burning building.

What's Next for NASA:
Artemis and Orion

The space program that landed the first man on the moon in 1969 was named Apollo, after the god from Greek mythology. The next upcoming lunar mission is named after Artemis, the twin sister of Apollo. This is a meaningful choice given that one aspect of the Artemis mission is to send the first woman to walk on the moon.

For the ARTEMIS mission, NASA scientists developed a new rocket, the most powerful in the world, called the SPACE LAUNCH SYSTEM (SLS). The SLS will transport the Orion spacecraft with four astronauts up to the moon, where they will search for water and other resources in previously unexplored areas.

Orion (similar to the spacecraft shown here) is designed to be capable of taking humans into deep space—to Mars or even an asteroid. It is similar to the Apollo spacecraft but larger and can carry four astronauts rather than three.

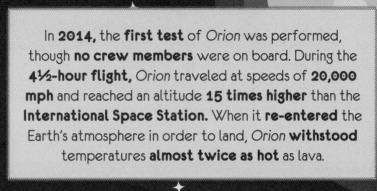

In **2014,** the **first test** of *Orion* was performed, though **no crew members** were on board. During the **4½-hour flight,** *Orion* traveled at speeds of **20,000 mph** and reached an altitude **15 times higher** than the **International Space Station.** When it **re-entered** the Earth's atmosphere in order to land, *Orion* **withstood** temperatures **almost twice as hot** as lava.

THE ARTEMIS PROGRAM, SET TO REACH THE MOON BY 2024, IS IMPORTANT BECAUSE IT AIMS TO ALLOW SCIENTISTS TO LEARN MORE ABOUT HUMANS ON THE MOON; RESEARCH THAT WILL BE USED TO POTENTIALLY ALLOW ASTRONAUTS TO TRAVEL FARTHER THAN HUMANS HAVE EVER TRAVELED BEFORE.

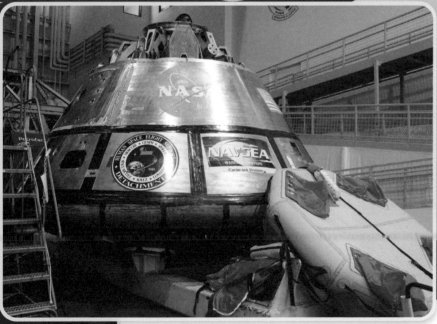

© Bambi L Dingman | Dreamstime.com

The Artemis program aims to land on the moon's south pole: an area where no human has ever walked.

Orion is designed to have advanced safety features for astronauts, such as life-support systems and other computers and electronics. When *Orion* returns to Earth, it will land in the water because it will travel at a very high speed. To help *Orion* land, scientists redesigned the parachutes to be stronger than previous versions because *Orion* will be traveling from an even greater distance: deep space.

Fun Facts about Mammals

Most mammals have whiskers on their cheeks, lips, or heads to help feel their way in the dark.

They have fur or hair to protect them and keep them warm.

Every mammal has a four-chambered heart. A mammal's circulating blood carries more oxygen than the blood of other animals.

Most mammals give birth to live babies (instead of laying eggs, for example).

They are warm-blooded animals, meaning they can survive in many climates and changing temperatures.

Each mammal has a cranium—a hard case made of bone and cartilage—that surrounds the brain. For high level thinking, mammals—and only mammals—have a neocortex in the brain.

They all have diaphragms, sheets of muscle that separate body parts: the heart and lungs are in the upper section, and the liver, stomach, kidneys, intestines, and reproductive organs are in the lower section.

Word Search

Mammals

Look for different kinds of mammals in the puzzle below. Circle the words going across, up and down, and diagonally. Some words may be backward!

ANTELOPE	GORILLA	POLAR BEAR
BUFFALO	HEDGEHOG	RHINOCEROS
DOLPHIN	LEOPARD	WEASEL
ELEPHANT	ORANGUTAN	ZEBRA

```
N V A G S V N B T R X S H R E
A E R Z D O U C A S I O E J I
T O X I R F R E E N O I D L I
U N F R F E B E O R Y U G A D
G W S A I R U M C E I A E N R
N H L N A X M P G O D V H W A
A O W L Z E B R A D N M O I P
R P O X U Y L A L L T I G W O
O P O D G L R E M B L I H L E
U U Y W Y F H E P S A I E R L
N I H P L O D I M H N S R Y O
F C R C O M H F T P A R F O F
U A J L P R O N H E U N E U G
S M Y O G H U O W Z I E T H X
J W A N T E L O P E U V L B R
```

Fossils

Fossils, the preserved remains of plants and animals, have been found mostly in sedimentary rocks. By studying fossils, scientists can learn all about prehistoric life.

THE LARGEST FOSSILS EVER FOUND BELONG TO DINOSAURS AND TREES. SOME DINOSAURS WERE OVER 130 FEET LONG!

Fossils are often bones but can also be things like teeth, wood, or shell. You can also find fossilized tracks, burrows, skin impressions, and even fossilized pieces of poop, which are called coprolites.

WHAT IS A "LIVING FOSSIL"?

A plant or animal that has survived almost unchanged for millions of years. A fish called coelacanth is a famous example. Until 1938, scientists believed that coelacanths had been extinct for 90 million years—then a living one was caught off the coast of South Africa. Sharks are also living fossils. They appeared more than 360 million years ago, long before dinosaurs.

In 1812, Mary Anning, a British fossil hunter, found the first ichthyosaurus (prehistoric fish) skeleton. Soon after, many skeletons of dinosaurs were discovered all over the world.

A PLANT FOSSIL IS FORMED WHEN PARTS OF THE PLANT ROT SLOWLY. THIS CAN HAPPEN IF THEY ARE COVERED WITH CLAY, MUD, OR SAND. SCIENTISTS ARE ABLE TO STUDY LEAVES, STEMS, ROOTS, AND FRUIT OF DIFFERENT TYPES OF PLANTS THROUGH FOSSIL REMAINS.

Scientists use carbon dating to tell how old something is. Using this method, they are able to date rocks to the beginning of Earth's formation, millions of years ago.

Ammonites are fossils of extinct squid-like animals that lived in shells in the sea.

Stromatolites are the oldest fossils: They are fossilized mats made by blue-green bacteria, also called cyanobacteria. You can see stromatolites today in the ocean off the coast of Western Australia.

Mudslides

What is a mudslide?

A mudslide or landslide, as its name suggests, is the downhill, sliding movement of mud and rock that usually starts on steep hills after a heavy rainstorm or rapid snowmelt.

Are mudslides dangerous?

Yes! As it slides, the mud can move trees, cars, and even large boulders. In the United States alone, mudslides cause 25 to 50 deaths each year.

ARE SOME AREAS MORE PRONE TO MUDSLIDES THAN OTHERS?

Yes. Areas at the bottom of steep slopes and places that have already had mudslides are more likely to experience one.

Are there any warning signs before a mudslide occurs?

Right before a mudslide occurs, you might hear some unusual sounds—such as trees cracking, a rumbling noise, or boulders knocking against each other.

Floods

WHAT IS A FLOOD?

Like a mudslide, a flood can be a natural disaster. Floods happen when water overflows onto normally dry land.

WHAT CAUSES A FLOOD?

There can be many reasons. Some common causes of natural flooding include heavy rainfall for an extended time, large amounts of snow melting rapidly, and ice jams blocking the flow of running water.

What are the dangers of a flood?

Floods can kill people and animals. They can destroy homes and office buildings.

WHAT IS A FLASH FLOOD?

Flash floods are one of the most dangerous kinds of floods. They are caused by heavy rainfall or large snowmelts. A flash flood can happen in less than a minute and tend to last less than six hours.

Ye Olde Medicine

Popular medical treatments and diagnoses during the Middle Ages (from the 5th century AD to the 15th century)

DOCTORS USED URINE CHARTS TO DIAGNOSE ILLNESSES. CERTAIN COLORS IN URINE INDICATED CERTAIN ILLNESSES.

Medical treatment was often decided by a person's astrological sign. For example, if a person was a Taurus, doctors were careful to avoid cutting the neck and throat area. For a Virgo, they would avoid opening the belly area.

Bloodletting was a popular treatment for many diseases. Doctors believed that certain diseases were caused by too much blood in the body, so "letting" some out was the obvious cure. If they needed to take a lot of blood, they would cut a vein. If they thought a small amount needed to come out, they would attach a leech to suck out the blood.

Many people of the Middle Ages believed that diseases such as smallpox and the plague were caused by sinful behavior. They thought the only cure was for the sinner to experience pain. Imagine this: Some people actually whipped themselves as a treatment. As you may have guessed, this didn't work!

Renaissance Medicine

THE RENAISSANCE period, from the 14th century to the 17th century, saw enormous growth in the arts and sciences. People were curious about the human body and began making scientific discoveries that replaced Middle Age thinking.

Great Renaissance artists, like **LEONARDO DA VINCI**, made drawings of the inside of the human body.

People used to believe the heart made blood from food and drink. During the Renaissance, they learned that the heart is a muscle that circulates blood throughout the body.

Medications, such as laudanum, were made. They were used to stop or reduce pain.

Ligatures were used to stop wounds from bleeding. This was the forerunner of today's stitches used to sew up cuts or incisions.

Anesthesia was used to help numb people so doctors could perform important surgeries.

High Tech

How does a cell phone work?

With radio signals and transmitters. "Cells" are the 10-square-mile units that cell phone companies divide cities and towns into. Each unit, or cell, has its own cell tower and base station. Signals from a cell phone transmit to the nearest cell tower and then to the phone of the person you're calling. If you use a cell phone in a moving vehicle, or walk a long distance, your phone's signal gets passed from one transmitter to the next, or from cell to cell.

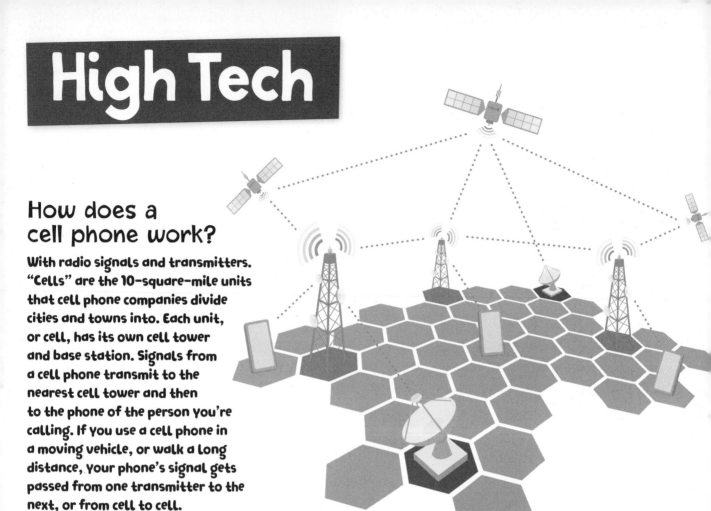

HOW DOES A DIGITAL CAMERA WORK?

In the blink of an eye. When you snap a photo, you focus the light that bounces off an image using the lens of your camera. A digital camera stores the image as a collection of pixels using a tiny microprocessor it has inside. There's no film in a digital camera, but the information stored in the microchip can be downloaded to a computer, which can then print out pictures or display them on screen.

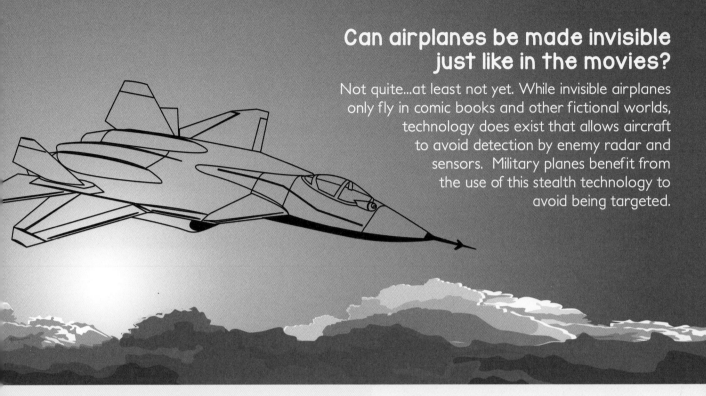

Can airplanes be made invisible just like in the movies?

Not quite...at least not yet. While invisible airplanes only fly in comic books and other fictional worlds, technology does exist that allows aircraft to avoid detection by enemy radar and sensors. Military planes benefit from the use of this stealth technology to avoid being targeted.

WHAT WILL CARS BE LIKE IN THE FUTURE?

Energy efficient and independent. It's likely cars that are powered by rechargeable batteries will become widely used, or cars may have engines that run on renewable fuels such as water or carbon dioxide. It's also possible that people will travel in cars that drive themselves! These autonomous vehicles would navigate highways, traffic, and parking lots, and still maintain safe speeds and distances from other cars.

OW DOES EMOTE CONTROL VORK?

Invisibly—with infrared light rays and electricity. If you want to change the channel on your TV, you press a button on the remote control unit and send a beam of infrared rays to the receiver unit in the TV. The beam contains a signal made of electrical pulses. The receiver detects the signal. Then it decodes the signal and changes the channel.

Fun Facts about Saturn

There are **250,000 miles** of rings around Saturn, made up of ice, dust, and rock. Saturn's rings are named alphabetically, in order of their discovery.

Saturn is known as the ringed planet, although Jupiter, Uranus, and Neptune have rings too. There are seven major rings around Saturn, but there could be thousands more!

One year on Saturn equals **29.42** Earth years!

Saturn has a **GREAT WHITE SPOT** that is really a huge **ATMOSPHERIC STORM.** It only appears about every **30 YEARS** or so.

Saturn

SATURN IS THE SECOND LARGEST PLANET IN THE SOLAR SYSTEM AFTER JUPITER.

CAN YOU STAND ON SATURN?

No. Unlike Earth, Saturn does not have a solid surface. It is a gas planet made up mostly of helium—the same type of gas used to fill up a balloon—and hydrogen.

What is the environment of Saturn like?

Winds near Saturn's equator blow at 1,100 miles per hour, making Saturn the windiest planet of all! The temperature is -218°F. Bundle up!

Saturn is the third brightest planet in the night sky.

Are Saturn's rings visible from Earth?

Sometimes we can see some of Saturn's rings clearly, and other times they are invisible. It depends which way the planet tilts as it rotates. Ring B is the largest and brightest ring around Saturn, so it's the easiest ring to see.

Saturn has more moons in its orbit than any other planet. Titan is Saturn's largest moon; it's very bright—and it's much bigger than the planet Mercury!

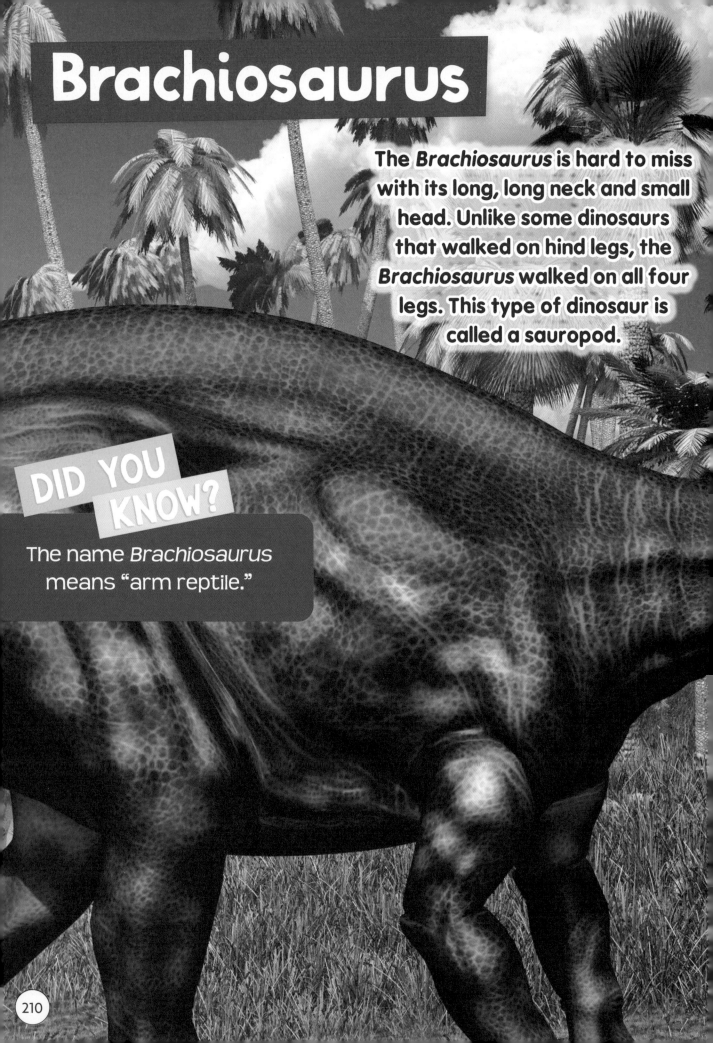

Brachiosaurus

The *Brachiosaurus* is hard to miss with its long, long neck and small head. Unlike some dinosaurs that walked on hind legs, the *Brachiosaurus* walked on all four legs. This type of dinosaur is called a sauropod.

DID YOU KNOW?

The name *Brachiosaurus* means "arm reptile."

Paleontologists once thought that *Brachiosaurus* spent most of its time underwater. They now know this is not true.

Brachiosaurus had a tiny head in comparison to the rest of its body. It could bring its head up very high, like a giraffe, to eat from tall trees.

BRACHIOSAURUS WAS SO **LARGE** IT HAD FEW, IF ANY, PREDATORS.

It is estimated that this dinosaur ate between **440 to 880 pounds** of vegetation a day— about the same weight as some **pine trees!**

The Water Cycle

Earth's surface is covered in reusable water. The water keeps circulating around and around in what we call the hydrologic, or water, cycle. The water cycle is made up of four main parts:

1 When the sun heats up water in rivers, lakes, and oceans, the water turns into steam or vapor. That steam or vapor, going into the air, is evaporation.

2 When the steam or water vapor gets cold and changes back into liquid, it forms clouds. This is condensation.

3 When so much water has condensed that it can no longer be held in the air, water falls back to Earth in the form of rain, hail, sleet, or snow. The precipitation will fall back into oceans, lakes, or rivers, or onto land.

4 Collection occurs on land when the precipitation soaks into the land and becomes water for plants and animals. The water that does not soak into the land will collect by going back to oceans, lakes, or rivers, and the water cycle begins all over again.

19th Century
Medicine

A British doctor named Edward Jenner discovered that by injecting a small amount of cowpox (a disease found in cows) into a person, he or she would become immune to smallpox.

A French chemist named Louis Pasteur developed the vaccine against rabies, saving people from otherwise deadly animal bites.

In the 1800s, coughing was a sign of tuberculosis (TB). Long ago, this disease was the leading cause of death in children from one to four years old. It was highly contagious, passed through the air from a person coughing. In 1882, a German doctor named ROBERT KOCH developed a way to actually see the tuberculosis bacteria. His developments made it possible for researchers to discover possible treatments.

This and That

What are the different states of matter?

Matter is every substance in the universe. It is anything that takes up space, and everything that exists is made of matter. Matter can be solid (like rock or wood), liquid (like water or oil), or gas (like air). Water can be all three states depending on the temperature.

Water is **SOLID** (ice) when its temperature is below 32°F.

Water is **LIQUID** when its temperature is between 32°F and 212°F.

Water turns to **GAS** (water vapor) when its temperature is higher than 212°F.

WHAT ARE GEODES?

Round hollow rocks lined on the inside with fascinating, often beautiful, crystal formations. The most common type of geode forms from gas bubbles that get stuck inside a certain type of lava flow. Over time, the lava hardens and the bubbles transform into cavities surrounded by rock exteriors. Sometimes, while the lava is still hardening, hot water filters into the cavity. Other times, over the course of millions of years, mineralized groundwater seeps in. Once the water is inside, crystals begin to grow—usually quartz. The exciting thing about geodes is you never know what they're like inside until you break them open!

Why are tall mountains often snowcapped?

When warm winds hit a mountain, they are forced upward where they cool. Then the moisture they carry forms clouds. The higher you go, the cooler and thinner the air. Warm air hitting a mountain creates the perfect conditions for snow to form and fall on the mountain's peak.

What would happen if there were no more plants in the world?

There would be no world as we know it. Plants are a necessary link in the cycle of nature that connects all living things. Photosynthesis supplies us with the oxygen we breathe. Plants are a source of food and shelter for many animals. Plants also keep the soil from blowing away in the wind.

WHERE IS THE VALLEY OF TEN THOUSAND SMOKES?

In Katmai National Monument, Alaska. One of the biggest volcanic eruptions in recorded history occurred here in 1912. Visitors to the valley four years later reported steam rising from tens of thousands of "smokes," or fumaroles—holes in the valley floor near the volcano.

Crafty Spacecrafts

The Russian spacecraft *Soyuz* launches from Kazakhstan and takes crews of up to three cosmonauts or astronauts to and from the International Space Station (ISS). There are multiple *Soyuz* spacecrafts, and one is docked at the ISS at all times—a sort of "life boat" in case of emergency.

One of the three parts of the *Soyuz* capsule is the Orbital Module, about the size of a large van, which is where the crew lives during orbit. The smaller Descent Module is where the controls are located, so the crew must sit there during takeoff. The journey from Earth to the ISS can take about six hours, depending on where the ISS is in orbit.

Launched in 2011, *Juno* is a spacecraft NASA designed to research Jupiter—a planet that took *Juno* five years to reach.

Juno's mission is not only to study Jupiter and its gaseous surface but also to gather data that will allow scientists to better understand how planets are made and change over time.

NAMED FOR THE ROMAN GODDESS AND WIFE OF THE GOD JUPITER, THE *JUNO* SPACECRAFT CARRIES SMALL LEGO® FIGURES REPRESENTING THE MYTHOLOGY OF THE SPACECRAFT'S NAME.

During its 37 planned orbits around Jupiter, *Juno* will measure the planet's magnetic and gravitational fields, and the amount of water and ammonia in the atmosphere, and it will take pictures of areas scientists seek to better understand, like the auroras in the north and south poles. At the end of its 37th orbit, *Juno* will enter Jupiter's atmosphere and blow up.

Extraterrestrial Info

AN EASY WAY TO UNDERSTAND THE SIZE DIFFERENCE BETWEEN EARTH AND THE SUN IS TO PICTURE THE SUN THE SIZE OF AN AVERAGE FRONT DOOR, AND EARTH THE SIZE OF A NICKEL IN COMPARISON.

It would take **100,000 light-years** to travel across the Milky Way galaxy.

The human footprints on the moon made back in July 1969 might be there forever—the lack of atmosphere on the moon means there is no erosion from wind or water, nor is there any volcanic activity. However, if a meteorite—even a tiny one—were to hit the moon in that location, it could easily erase the footprints.

Scientists found a planet using the Hubble Space Telescope, located 63 light-years away, that has temperatures of over 1,800°F, around 4,300 mph winds, and rainstorms of glass!

The Oort Cloud is a large spherical shell that surrounds the planets, sun, and the Kuiper Belt objects. Made of icy comet-like objects, some as large or larger than mountains, the Oort Cloud acts as a bubble around our solar system.

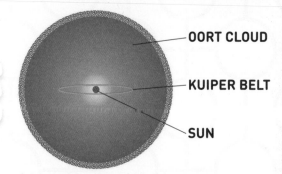

OORT CLOUD

KUIPER BELT

SUN

"Planet X" is a mysterious scientific discovery: According to mathematical calculations by scientists at Caltech, there might be another planet the size of Neptune in our solar system. It has not yet been observed, and there is debate among scientists about whether it exists. Astronomers continue to use advanced technology, like powerful telescopes, to try to confirm its existence or to find another explanation for the altered orbits of tiny objects in the Kuiper Belt thought to be caused by this "Planet X."

Making Words

Inter-speller

The word "planet" comes from various root words, including the Greek *asters planetai*, or "wandering stars."

Look at the word below. How many words, of three or more letters, can you make using only the letters in PLANET? Fill out your answers on the lines below.

PLANET

_____   _____

_____   _____

_____   _____

_____   _____

_____   _____

_____   _____

_____   _____

_____   _____

Pollutants and the Environment

WHAT IS AIR POLLUTION?

Air that has been tainted by toxic (poisonous) chemicals. Many such chemicals are given off when fossil fuels are burned—by car or truck engines, for instance, or by factories or power plants. Air pollution contributes to water pollution when solid particles of harmful chemicals rise through the air to mix with water particles in clouds, then fall as rain.

WHAT IS ORGANIC GARDENING?

A way of growing plants without using chemical pesticides and fertilizers. "Organic" means using natural food or fertilizers rather than chemical ones. Organic fertilizers, such as compost (rotted plant material) or fish meal, are used to enrich the soil. Instead of any insecticide, an organic farmer may use ladybugs to get rid of problem insects. Organic gardening grows crops without hurting the environment.

Who was Rachel Carson?

Rachel Carson (1907-1964) was a marine biologist and environmentalist. In 1962, her book *Silent Spring* was published and gained widespread attention. It made many people aware, for the first time, of how humans were polluting the environment with insecticides. Carson wrote other nature books, but *Silent Spring* is regarded as her masterpiece—the book that launched the modern environmental movement throughout the world.

How can pesticides harm birds?

If a bird eats animals that have been exposed to pesticides, the chemicals stay in the bird's body and become concentrated there. Sometimes chemicals cause a bird to lay eggs with shells that break easily, preventing the eggs from hatching. If the bird absorbs too high a level of the chemicals, it may be poisoned and die. Pesticides almost wiped out peregrine falcons and bald eagles in the eastern United States.

What are fossil fuels?

Fuels made from the remains of plants that lived millions of years ago. Natural gas, coal, and oil are all fossil fuels.

What is harming the ozone layer?

Industrial chemicals called chlorofluorocarbons (CFCs) are the biggest culprit. When CFCs get into Earth's upper atmosphere, they break up to form chlorine monoxide and other chemicals that damage the ozone there.

Earth's ozone layer is an important protection against the sun's ultraviolet rays, which are harmful to humans and other forms of life. To protect the ozone layer, many companies now use less-harmful chemicals in aerosol sprays and refrigerants, the main source of CFCs.

Fun Facts about Uranus

Uranus is a beautiful blue-green color. This coloring comes from its atmosphere, consisting mostly of methane.

Uranus has 27 moons. The largest moon, Titania, has a diameter that's about half the size of our moon's diameter.

AFTER SATURN, URANUS HAS THE MOST DRAMATIC RINGS. SCIENTISTS BELIEVE THEY WERE FORMED RECENTLY.

Uranus

One day on Uranus, a full rotation of the planet, is 17 Earth hours long.

Uranus is the seventh planet from the sun and the third of the gas giant planets. Uranus is a giant ball of gas and liquid, and the farthest planet that can be seen without a telescope from Earth.

Uranus has only been visited once, and that was in 1986 by NASA's Voyager 2.

Uranus is the coldest planet in the solar system. It is about -155°F, and the strong winds (up to 188 miles per hour) keep the temperature cold all the time! Brrrrr.

UNLIKE OTHER PLANETS, URANUS ROTATES ON ITS SIDE, SO AT ANY GIVEN TIME ONE OF ITS POLES IS POINTED TOWARD THE SUN. THIS MEANS THAT EACH POLE EXPERIENCES 42 EARTH YEARS OF DAY, FOLLOWED BY 42 EARTH YEARS OF NIGHT IN ONE FULL URANUS YEAR.

All about Animals

DUCKS ARE HEAVIER THAN WATER, SO WHY DON'T THEY SINK?

Air trapped in ducks' feathers and held in their lungs makes them light enough to float. When a duck wants to dive under water for food, it exhales some air from its lungs to make it easier to sink. Waterproof feathers may also help ducks float.

Why do houseflies walk on food?

To find out what it tastes like. Houseflies have taste buds on their feet. If they like what they taste, they sponge saliva on the food until it dissolves, because flies can only consume liquids. Then they slurp it up!

Where and why do some people celebrate Buzzard Day?

In Hinckley, Ohio, the first Sunday after March 15 is Buzzard Day. Buzzard Day celebrates the return of migrating buzzards—actually, turkey vultures—that spend each summer near Hinckley. The first birds usually reach the area around March 15 each year.

Why might you call the hognose snake and the opossum "animal actors"?

When attacked, they often play dead, because most predators are likely to lose interest in unmoving prey and leave. The opossum lies on its side, usually refusing to move even if poked or prodded. The hognose snake rolls onto its back and lets its tongue fall out of its mouth. When the coast is clear, each "actor" wakes up and dashes off.

Are Komodo dragons the kind of dragons found in fairy tales?

No. Komodo dragons are giant lizards that live on Komodo Island and a few other Indonesian islands in Southeast Asia. Komodo dragons can weigh up to 300 pounds and grow as long as 10 feet. They are so big that they can eat a wild goat whole! A Komodo dragon can live to be about 100 years old.

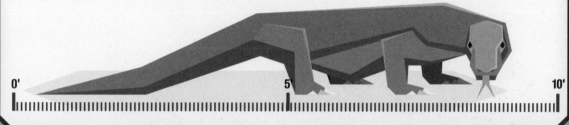

0'   5'   10'

WHAT ARE ZOOS?

Zoos are public and private parks where animals are kept so that people can observe and learn about them. Zoos educate the public about animal behavior and about conservation. Few people have the chance to see wild animals in their natural surroundings (such as monkeys in tropical rain forests or zebras in African savannas). Zoos also help to protect animals that are in danger of extinction.

Who created the first zoo?

The first zoo was created in the 12th century BC by King Wen of China. It was called "The Garden of Intelligence." King Wen collected different animals from across his empire to live in his zoo. Today, the best zoos want their animals to feel at home, so they create environments similar to an animal's natural surroundings.

ZOO

Bodies of Water

The Pacific Ocean

This is the world's largest ocean. The Pacific covers almost half of Earth's surface and holds almost half of its water. The coastal land that surrounds the ocean is called the Pacific Rim.

THE ATLANTIC OCEAN

The Atlantic contains about 25% of Earth's water. It was the first ocean to be crossed by ship and airplane.

THE INDIAN OCEAN

The Indian Ocean covers about 20% of Earth's surface. It is the warmest ocean in the world.

THE SOUTHERN OCEAN

The Southern Ocean is located around the South Pole, across the Antarctic Circle in the Southern Hemisphere off Antarctica. It is also known as the Antarctic Ocean.

The Arctic Ocean

The Arctic Ocean is located around the North Pole across the Arctic Circle. It's the smallest and shallowest of the five oceans.

RIVERS

A river is a large natural stream of running water. Most rivers start on a mountain or hill where rainwater or melted ice and snow form a narrow stream. The stream often joins with other bodies of water to form larger streams, or tributaries.

Tributaries feed into a river that can take a winding path around hills and through valleys until it reaches the sea.

The highest end of a river usually moves quickly, carrying dirt, pebbles, and rocks.

Some rivers—like the Roe River in Montana—are short, while others—like the Nile in Africa—are very long.

At its center, a river moves a bit slower and becomes wider. When it gets close to the sea, it moves even slower and drops sediment. As a river enters the sea, it leaves behind much of the dirt and rocks it has carried, building up a small landmass called a delta.

LAKES

Holes and dips in the land often fill with rainwater. These holes are called lakes.

The largest freshwater lake in the world is LAKE SUPERIOR in North America.

The largest saltwater lake is the CASPIAN SEA, which is found in Asia.

The Human Body in Space

The Human Research Program at NASA is focused on understanding what happens to a body that goes to space, particularly over a longer period of time. This research is especially important for preparing humans to travel to Mars.

HUMAN ORGANS are used to set amounts of gravity, so the **microgravity** in the International Space Station presents a brand-new experience for the human body. While the body is able to adapt, some astronauts experience changes in their body upon their return to Earth, such as loss of muscle mass.

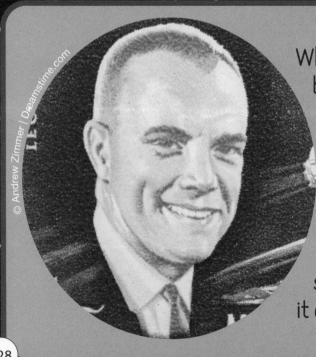

When **JOHN GLENN** became the first American to orbit Earth, he was given applesauce to eat in a toothpaste-like tube, chosen by scientists on the ground to test if Glenn's body would swallow the food and move it down to his stomach.

In 2019, NASA released their results of the three-year study of the Kelly twin brothers. Scott Kelly, an astronaut who spent almost a year in space, experienced many biological changes, such as DNA mutations in cells and new signals produced by his immune system during orbit, compared to his twin brother Mark, also an astronaut, on Earth. Some changes did not last when Scott returned to Earth, but others did. This study, the first of its kind, is important as astronauts look to spend more time in space as well as travel greater distances.

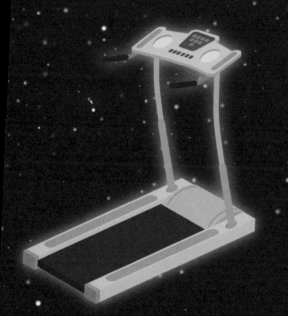

Because time spent in space results in bone and muscle loss, astronauts must be careful to stay fit and strong—exercising an average of two hours every day. The exercise equipment—including pieces like a treadmill, a weight-lifting machine, and a bicycle—is specially designed to work in microgravity.

Just like humans on Earth, astronauts should get eight hours of sleep every night. Though microgravity means astronauts can sleep in any position, it also means they can float around. To sleep, they use sleeping bags attached to a small crew cabin, a personal area just big enough for one.

Being Human

HOW DID THE TOOTH FAIRY LEGEND START?

Dr. Rosemary Wells, who researched the tooth fairy for more than 20 years, said that losing baby teeth has been important in all cultures, even ancient ones. It's a symbol of "leaving babyhood and entering childhood." Some countries have invented magical animals instead of a fairy. The United States is the only country with a tooth fairy who exchanges money for teeth! Dr. Wells opened a Tooth Fairy Museum in Illinois with all kinds of objects, even a singing tooth fairy toothbrush.

WHAT ARE TEARS FOR?

Tears are cleaning fluid for the eye. They come from the lacrimal glands, which sit above the outer edge of each eye. Every time you blink, they cover your eye and wash away dirt and germs. When you cry, tears may help you get rid of extra chemicals that build up in your body.

Why can you see your breath when it's really cold?

When you exhale in cold weather, the water vapor in your warm breath hits the cold air and condenses into tiny water droplets. Presto: an instant mini-cloud!

DOES HAY CAUSE HAY FEVER?

Not really. The sneezes and sniffles of hay fever are an allergic reaction to pollen and mold in the air. Allergies make the body's defense systems react to harmless substances as if they were dangerous.

While many people who suffer from hay fever feel worse in spring, summer, and early fall, others experience symptoms year-round.

If your skin is always RENEWING itself, how can you have a scar for life?

Your skin is like a rug woven of many fibers. If a cut isn't too wide, skin cells reweave the rug just like new. However, if the cut edges are far apart, skin cells can't bridge the gap. Fibroblasts—cells that make bigger, tougher strands of skin—fill the space. This becomes a permanent scar.

WHY CAN I SEE MYSELF IN A MIRROR?

Everything you see comes from light rays that bounce off objects and bounce back to your eyes. A mirror is glass with a shiny chemical coating on the back. When you stand in front of a mirror, light rays bounce off your body onto the mirror's coating. Then the rays reflect, or bounce back, to your eyes. What you are is what you see—it's your reflection.

The Body's Oddities

What does it mean to be double-jointed?

Not what you may think. Every elbow, knee, ankle, and shoulder is a spot where two bones meet and a joint connects them. Fingers and toes have many joints. Some people can bend these joints in pretty amazing ways, but they've got the same number of joints as the rest of us. They're just more flexible.

WHY DO PEOPLE HAVE STRAIGHT, WAVY, OR CURLY HAIR?

As a strand of hair grows, it squeezes through a tiny hole called a follicle. The shape of a person's follicles makes hair straight, wavy, or curly. Think of a toothpaste tube: If the opening weren't round but shaped like a square or a star instead, the stream of toothpaste would look completely different. Straight hair grows out of round follicles, waves from oval follicles, and tight, round curls spring from square follicles!

Why do we LAUGH?

Because it feels good and helps us relax. What we laugh at is another story. You could giggle yourself silly over something that your friend thinks is stupid, boring, or even insulting. Once you get started, it's hard to stop: Laughter is one of the automatic responses your body takes care of on its own. Your stomach tenses up. Your face scrunches up. Tears squeeze out of your tear glands. When it's over, **YOU FEEL GOOD!**

HOW DO WE GROW?

Slowly. The pituitary gland, located in the brain just behind the bridge of the nose, sets the pace. One of the hormones, or chemicals, it releases stimulates growth, causing our cells to divide and multiply. The more cells there are, the more of us there is! Scientists aren't sure why we stop growing, but fortunately there seems to be a limit!

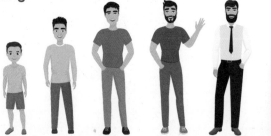

Underwater Matching
Fishy Trio

The Great Barrier Reef, located off the coast of Australia, is the world's largest reef system, made up of 900 islands and over 2,900 individual reefs. Many different species of animals live there, including 215 species of birds, 17 species of sea snakes, 30 species of whales, dolphins, and porpoises, and over 1,500 species of fish.

There are many different types of fish under the sea! Look at the underwater scene and circle the 3 fish that are exactly the same.

Answers on page 311

Out of this World

The first image of a black hole was captured on April 10, 2019. Scientists used the Event Horizon Telescope, a group of eight telescopes, over the course of five days. That black hole is located about **55 MILLION LIGHT-YEARS FROM EARTH.**

THERE ARE MORE STARS IN THE SKY THAN GRAINS OF SAND ON EARTH.

Normal matter—Earth and everything humans have ever observed—represents less than 5% of the universe; dark matter—an invisible substance in the universe—represents around 25%; dark energy—an invisible force in the universe—represents around 70%.

The core of the sun is about 27 million degrees Fahrenheit.

About 99.8% of the mass of the full solar system is made up by

THE SUN

A CONSTELLATION IS A RECOGNIZABLE PATTERN OF STARS, WHILE AN ASTERISM IS A PATTERN OF STARS THAT IS PART OF A BIGGER CONSTELLATION. FOR EXAMPLE, THE BIG DIPPER IS AN ASTERISM, NOT A CONSTELLATION, AS IT IS THE BEST-KNOWN PART OF THE CONSTELLATION URSA MAJOR.

Body Systems

Your body parts all work together in systems, or groups, of organs to help you do things like move, digest food, and breathe.

HERE ARE 6 OF THE MAIN SYSTEMS:

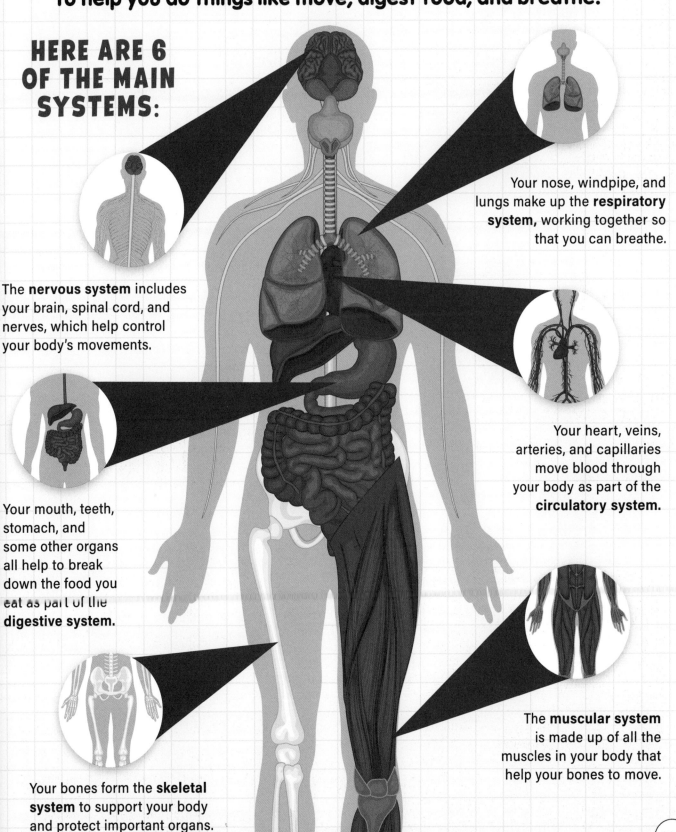

Your nose, windpipe, and lungs make up the **respiratory system,** working together so that you can breathe.

The **nervous system** includes your brain, spinal cord, and nerves, which help control your body's movements.

Your heart, veins, arteries, and capillaries move blood through your body as part of the **circulatory system.**

Your mouth, teeth, stomach, and some other organs all help to break down the food you eat as part of the **digestive system.**

The **muscular system** is made up of all the muscles in your body that help your bones to move.

Your bones form the **skeletal system** to support your body and protect important organs.

Watered Down

Where is the deepest lake in the world?

Siberia, a region in Russia, is home to Lake Baikal, the world's deepest lake. Its lowest point plunges more than a mile below the surface—5,315 feet.

Where is the longest river in the world?

The world's longest river is the Nile, which runs through 11 countries in northeastern Africa, including Egypt and Sudan. It is about 4,160 MILES LONG.

WHAT IS DEW?

On cool, cloud-free nights, if the temperature of the ground and other surfaces drops low enough, warm air cools down, condensing moisture contained in it. That moisture collects on cool surfaces in droplets of water called dew.

HOW DOES A GLACIER FORM?

Glaciers form at high elevations when more snow falls than melts, causing it to build up. The pressure of all that snow causes glacial ice to form. The ice becomes so heavy that the glaciers begin to move. Most glaciers travel slowly—only about a foot a day. A glacier can grow to be more than a mile thick—and even the size of a small island or continent! In fact, 98% of the continent of Antarctica is covered by a glacier.

HOW CAN WATER CREATE ELECTRICITY?

The force of water falling over a dam can power machines that make electricity. Here's how it works:

Water falls from a great height onto the paddles of a turbine—think of a pinwheel spinning when you blow on it.

These giant metal turbines whirl up to 750 revolutions per minute. They provide the mechanical energy that rotates the magnet in an electrical generator. The generator uses magnets and copper wire to create electrical energy. This electricity travels through wires to the light bulb in your lamp.

WHICH WATERFALL HAS THE MOST WATER?

Khone Falls, in Laos, a country in Asia. Its flow of 2 million gallons of water per second gives it the greatest volume of any waterfall in the world. That is nearly twice the volume of Niagara Falls, which has the greatest volume of any US waterfall.

TSUNAMI TRIVIA

- A tsunami is not just one big wave. It's a series of waves called a wave train.

- The time period between waves can be anywhere from just a few minutes to 2 hours.

- In the deepest part of the ocean, tsunami waves are usually only 1 to 3 feet tall.

- The states in the United States at greatest risk for tsunamis are Hawaii, Alaska, Washington, Oregon, and California.

- Tsunami waves can travel at the speed of a jet plane, over 600 miles per hour.

All About Sharks

Scary movies and news reports have made people frightened of shark attacks, but believe it or not, most sharks are scared of people and try to avoid them when they can.

EXPERT SWIMMERS!

Sharks swim by bending from side to side.

First comes the head, then the body, followed by the long tail—all pushing the shark through ocean waters.

Time to moisturize! Shark skin feels like rough sandpaper.

MR. FIX IT!

The hammerhead shark has a head that actually looks like the head of a hammer!

SHARK ATTACK!

The sharks that are most likely to attack people are tiger sharks and great white sharks.

CRUNCH!

Just before they bite, sharks tip their noses up and thrust their teeth forward. They can smell blood from hundreds of yards away.

DENTAL DISASTERS!

A shark's teeth are super strong: They can chomp through just about anything. They quickly get blunt, though, and fall out, only to be replaced by new ones.

Fun Facts
about Neptune

NEPTUNE IS THE ONLY PLANET THAT CANNOT BE SEEN WITH THE NAKED EYE, WITHOUT A TELESCOPE.

What are the winds like on Neptune? Neptune's winds blow just over 1,000 miles per hour, making it one of the windiest planets in the solar system.

WHAT IS NEPTUNE'S GREAT DARK SPOT?

The spot indicates an atmospheric storm, a cyclone rotating in a counterclockwise direction. The Great Dark Spot seen by *Voyager 2* was about the size of the planet Earth and has since disappeared, and two other spots have also come and gone as seen through the Hubble Space Telescope.

Why is Neptune's atmosphere blue?

Neptune is made of hydrogen, helium, and methane. The methane lies over the planet's thick cloud cover and reflects blue hues. However, scientists do not know why Neptune is so much brighter than Uranus, which has a similar blue atmosphere.

240

Neptune

What is Neptune like?

Neptune is the farthest planet from the sun and the smallest of the gas giants. It's a bright blue planet. A 1989 visit by the spacecraft *Voyager 2* and observations by the Hubble Space Telescope showed similarities to Uranus: strong winds, many dark and light spots on the surface, rings, and moons.

All of the planets in our solar system, except Earth, are named after Greek and Roman gods. Neptune is named after the Roman god of the sea because of the planet's blueish color.

How many moons does Neptune have?

Neptune has 13 known moons. The moons are all named after gods and creatures in Greek mythology. Neptune's largest moon is Triton, named after the Greek demigod of the sea.

How many rings does Neptune have?

Neptune has six known rings made of microscopic particles or dust. The outermost ring, the Adams ring, has three arcs named Liberty, Equality, and Fraternity.

Neptune is the first and only planet discovered by using mathematical calculations rather than observations of the sky.

Because of their orbits, Neptune and Pluto sometimes trade places and become closer to the sun. From 1979 to 1999, Neptune was farther from the sun than Pluto. Now, Pluto is farther from the sun—and will stay that way for the next 230 or so years.

One year on Neptune is the same as 165 Earth years.

Super Supernovae

Most stars fade when they die, but supernovae are stars that explode instead—creating an extreme, bright blast that can be seen across the universe.

There are two types of supernovae. The first happens between two stars orbiting the same point. One of the stars, a white dwarf, takes matter from the other star—so much that the white dwarf eventually explodes. The second happens when a star runs out of fuel and its core collapses, causing the star to explode—signaling the end of that star's life.

THE SUN MAY SEEM BIG, BUT IT IS NOT LARGE ENOUGH TO EVER BECOME A SUPERNOVA.

The ASASSN-15lh SUPERNOVA (pronounced "assassin") is the brightest supernova discovered so far. It is 200 times brighter than most other supernovae and a staggering 570 billion times brighter than the sun!

Supernovae are extremely rare.

Scientists believe they occur within the Milky Way only about two or three times a century.

THE BLAST FROM A SUPERNOVA PRODUCES A LOT OF THE MATERIAL IN THE UNIVERSE AND SENDS CLOUDS OF GAS AND DUST INTO SPACE, WHICH HELP CREATE NEW STARS.

In 2011, at age 10, Canadian Kathryn Gray became the youngest person to discover a supernova. Gray was looking through images sent to her dad, an amateur astronomer, when she spotted the object 240 million light-years away.

Prehistory

Prehistory usually means the time before 3500 BC—when people first started to record their lives and surroundings. To learn what Earth was like in prehistoric times, scientists study fossils and rocks. Based on these studies, scientists have divided prehistory into different eras (time periods) based on which life forms existed when.

Precambrian Period
4.5 billion to 570 million years ago

Earth forms, 4.5 billion years ago; first signs of life on Earth, 3.8 billion years ago

Cambrian Period
570 to 510 million years ago

Many kinds of life appear in the oceans, including sponges; fish (first animals with backbones) appear

Ordovician Period
510 to 440 million years ago

First coral reefs to appear; also, nautiloids—squid-like creatures with long, pointy shells

Silurian Period
440 to 408 million years ago

Plants begin to grow on land; fish appear in freshwater; millipedes and scorpions move onto land

Devonian Period
408 to 362 million years ago

Sharks and rays appear; first seed-producing plants; first forests; amphibians evolve from fish

Carboniferous Perio
362 to 290 million years ago

Time of great forests; first winge insects; first reptiles

Permian Period
290 to 251 million years ago

Reptiles dominate on land; period ends in a massive extinction

Cretaceous Period
145 to 65 million years ago

Dinosaurs still dominate; first flowering plants; period ends in extinction of dinosaurs, marine reptiles, and other animals and plants

Triassic Period
251 to 199 million years ago

Pangaea (Earth's single landmass) splits; first dinosaurs and mammals

Pangaea

Tertiary Period
65 to 1.65 million years ago

Australopithecus, ancestor to humans, appears (about 4 million years ago)

Jurassic Period
199 to 145 million years ago

Dinosaurs dominate Earth; mammals remain small; first birds appear

Quaternary Period
1.65 million years ago to present

Humans evolve into the body type we have today (about 200,000 years ago)

Prehistoric People

Six million years ago, our prehistoric human ancestors started to evolve larger brains than all the other primates.

Australopithecus appeared in Africa four million years ago. It is the earliest known biped, which means it was the first human to walk on two legs. The most complete Australopithecus fossil ever found is named Lucy!

HOMO HABILIS (ABOUT 2.5 MILLION YEARS AGO) CARVED TOOLS AND BUILT SHELTERS.

Homo erectus (about 1.75 million years ago) had a bigger brain, better tools, and probably started to use fire.

Most scientists think that the first modern humans, Homo sapiens, spread out from Africa about 100,000 years ago, eventually replacing Neanderthals, who appeared in Europe about 130,000 years ago.

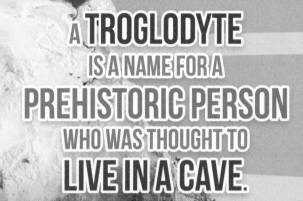

A **TROGLODYTE** IS A NAME FOR A **PREHISTORIC PERSON** WHO WAS THOUGHT TO **LIVE IN A CAVE.**

In prehistoric times, caves made excellent shelters for people. Scientists study caves and sometimes find places where bones were left or fires were lit. They can learn a lot about ancient civilizations by studying caves.

FIRE STARTERS

Cave dwellers probably learned about fire by observing nature—blazing hot lava, for instance, or bolts of lightning. They probably started fires by striking flints (a type of rock) together to create a spark. Some ancient peoples twirled a hard, pointed stick between their hands while pressing its point into a piece of softer wood, causing enough friction to start a fire.

Pteranodon

Is it a bird? Is it a plane? No, it's a flying reptile called *Pteranodon*. It is not actually a dinosaur, but it did live among the dinosaurs. Even though it could fly, it did not have feathers like a bird. When *Pteranodon* wasn't flying, it walked around on all four legs.

The *Pteranodon* had keen eyesight to help it catch its prey.

The Pteranodon's wings were larger than any bird alive today.

PTERANODON WAS NOT A FIGHTER. IT COULD PROBABLY FLY AWAY FROM MOST OF ITS ENEMIES.

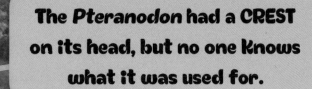

The *Pteranodon* had a CREST on its head, but no one knows what it was used for.

DID YOU KNOW?

The *Pteranodon* had no teeth! Scientists believe that *Pteranodons* used their long slender beaks to catch fish near the surface of the inland seas.

Many people think modern birds are very **distant relatives** of *Pteranodons*, but they're **not**. Modern birds probably came from **two-legged** dinosaurs, many of which were covered in **feathers**.

Animal Instincts

Why do birds sing?

To send other birds a message. Males do most of the singing. "This is my territory" seems to be the most common message. It may sound like a sweet song to us, but to other birds, it sounds like, "Keep out!"

Why are vultures good to have around?

Vultures are nature's cleanup crew. Experts believe that vultures living in Africa eat more meat than all other predators combined. Without vultures, rotting animal carcasses would spread disease, not to mention really stink things up!

For which animal were the Canary Islands named?

Dogs! The Latin word for dog is *canis*. Early explorers called the islands Canaria after the big, ferocious wild dogs they found living there. Canary birds, also found there, were named after the island—not the other way around.

WHAT IS THE ONLY KIND OF BIRD THAT CAN FLY UPSIDE DOWN?

The hummingbird—but not for long periods of time. Hummingbirds also fly backward to pull their beaks out of flowers. Like helicopters, they fly up and down, hover, or zip away at speeds of more than 60 miles per hour. To do all this, hummingbirds flap their wings 50 TO 75 TIMES A SECOND!

DO ALL TIGERS LIVE IN WARM JUNGLES?

No. The Siberian tiger, largest of all cats, lives in the Amur-Ussuri region of Siberia, Russia—not to mention northern China and Korea—which is covered with snow much of the year. To survive winter, the tiger grows an extra layer of fat.

How did guinea pigs get their name?

They were probably originally called Guiana (gee-AH-nuh) pigs because they make noises and movements that are a bit like those of regular pigs, and because Dutch traders found them in Dutch Guiana (now the independent country of Suriname) on South America's Caribbean coast. The animals' name eventually evolved into guinea pig.

Medicine in the 1900s

WHAT IS ABO BLOOD TYPING?

In 1901, a scientist named Karl Landsteiner developed the ABO system of blood typing. He described the importance of receiving compatible blood during transfusions. His system classified all human blood by types: A, B, AB, and O. In 1907, the first successful transfusion using Landsteiner's system took place.

Do you know your blood type?

AB

Who was Dr. Paul Dudley White?

He was one of America's first cardiologists, a doctor specializing in the heart. Dr. White was one of the first doctors to use the electrocardiograph machine to diagnose heart disease.

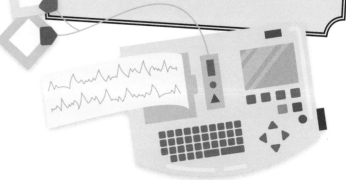

WHEN WAS INSULIN FIRST USED TO TREAT DIABETES?

INSULIN

In 1922, insulin became the treatment for diabetes. Back then, it had to be frequently injected by needle to be effective. Today, many advances, including a portable pump and oral medicine, can be used to administer insulin instead.

Which vaccines were developed in the 1900s?

In 1923, the diphtheria vaccine was developed. The pertussis vaccine came in 1926, and the tuberculosis shot followed in 1927. The vaccine for Yellow Fever was created in 1953, and tetanus in 1927. The flu shot came in 1945, and later, during the 1960s and '70s, vaccines for measles, mumps, rubella, and pneumonia were first used. These vaccines have eliminated many diseases and saved lives.

Medicine Today

In recent decades, advances in medicine have dramatically improved the health and life expectancy of people everywhere. Here are some of the big ones:

Improvements in trauma care (emergency treatment after an accident) have saved the lives of millions. Back in World War II, 30% of Americans injured in combat died. In the wars in Iraq and Afghanistan, only about 10% of those injured have died, due to advancements in trauma surgery.

In the recent past, patients with heart problems almost always needed heart surgery and a fair amount of time in the hospital. Today, using tiny tools and devices, doctors are able to repair many heart problems, sending patients home from the hospital in just a day or two.

Smoking bans in many public places, such as restaurants and theaters, in large cities all across the country have cut down on the amount of heart attacks people suffer and eliminated the risks of secondhand smoke to nonsmokers.

Thanks to free public health information online, people are better able to research information, stay up-to-date, and help themselves stay healthy.

Bugs and Birds

Why don't SPIDERS get STUCK in their own WEBS?

They avoid the sticky sections. Some spiders use dry silk for the web spokes, then lay down a circular pattern of sticky silk around it. The spider runs along the dry silk. If a leg does happen to stick, the spider uses its saliva to dissolve the glue.

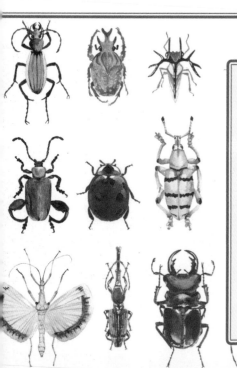

How many kinds of beetles are there?

The largest group of insects—by far—are beetles. Scientists know of about 300,000 different species of beetle, and there probably are many more yet to be identified. The biggest bunch in the beetle world is the weevil family—more than 500,000 species strong!

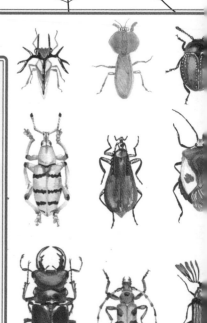

WHY DO MOTHS CIRCLE AROUND BRIGHT LIGHTS?

Night-flying moths navigate by staying at a constant angle to the moon. If they stick with the moon, they fly In a straight line every time. When they see artificial lights, they get confuse and try navigating by them instead, but it doesn't work nearly as well! To keep the ligh at the same angle, the moth must keep changing direction. It ends up flying in ever-smaller circles around the light.

Can all birds fly?

Not penguins, although they are expert swimmers. Not big birds, either. The shape and weight of giant birds like the African ostrich, South American rhea, and Australian emu prevent them from becoming airborne.

What is the difference between honeybees and wasps?

They belong to the same family, Apoidea, but there are many differences, aside from how they look. Honeybees live in hives. Some wasps build a nest out of "paper," which they make by chewing on wood and passing it through their bodies. Another difference is that honeybees collect the sweet nectar from flowers to make honey. Wasps make a meal of other insects. Also, if a honeybee stings, it loses its stinger and dies. Not the wasp: it stings and lives to sting again. One more difference. Honeybees live through the winter. Wasps, alas, do not.

Does it hurt a woodpecker to hammer on a tree?

No. Woodpeckers are hardheaded. They have thick skulls that can take the banging and strong neck muscles that absorb the shock.

What happened to passenger pigeons?

About 200 years ago, some 3 to 5 billion passenger pigeons lived in North America. They were overhunted by humans, however, and became extinct. The last passenger pigeon, named Martha, died in 1914. This may have been the only time in history when humans witnessed the precise moment of a species' extinction.

255

Fill-in Puzzle

Photosynthesis Phonics

Why do leaves change colors—reds, yellows, and oranges—in the fall? As the seasons change, temperatures get cooler and daylight decreases, which causes trees to produce less chlorophyll. With less chlorophyll, and eventually none at all, the other pigments in the leaf become visible—leading to an array of vibrant autumn colors. Climate change is impacting the changing leaves, as changes to precipitation and temperature impact the length of the colorful fall season.

Use the words at the bottom of the page to fill in the blanks in the puzzle.

4 Letters	5 Letters	6 Letters	7 Letters	8 Letters	11 Letters
Food	Green	Oxygen	Pigment	Organism	Chlorophyll
Fuel	Plant	Energy	Natural	Sunlight	
Cell		Carbon	Dioxide		
		Breath	Glucose		

Seasons

Do all trees change color in autumn?

No. Trees that change color with the season are called deciduous. Trees that stay green all year round are called evergreen. Which trees are which may depend on where you live. A species of trees that changes color and loses its leaves in autumn in a cool, northern climate may stay green and leafy all year long in a tropical area, where it is always warm and moist.

What makes seasons change?

Earth is tilted on its axis and keeps that tilt as it moves around the sun. When the northern half is tilted toward the sun, it has long, warm summer days, while the south has the short, cool winter days. On the other side of the sun, the positions are reversed, giving the north winter and the south summer.

Where do butterflies go in the winter?

When the weather starts to get chilly, some butterflies, such as the monarch, migrate to warmer places. Butterflies that stay in cold areas hibernate through the winter, after they lay eggs. The eggs hatch, and the offspring spend the winter as caterpillars or in cocoons, where the transformation from caterpillar to butterfly occurs.

What do snowshoe rabbits and ptarmigan do in spring and fall?

Change colors. These animals live in the far north, where winters are long and snowy. As winter approaches, the animals' coloring gradually changes from a mottled brown to a snowy white that blends better with snow. In the spring, it changes back to brown.

Nebulae

Nebulae are large clouds of gas and dust in space, sometimes caused by a dying star exploding. Other times, nebulae are areas where new stars are starting to form.

NEBULAE EXIST IN INTERSTELLAR SPACE, OR THE SPACE BETWEEN THE STARS.

There are two main visual classes of nebulae: DARK and BRIGHT. Dark nebulae cover the stars beyond them, creating dark patches, while bright nebulae emit their own light like a glowing surface.

The term "nebula" comes from the Latin word for "cloud."

The first record of a nebula observation dates back to 150 CE, when Ptolemy, an ancient mathematician, geographer, and astronomer, observed a group of stars that he described as "nebulous."

In the 19th century, the Herschel family of astronomers—William, his sister Caroline, and his son John—did significant work documenting nebulae and galaxies. Together in England, William and Caroline made three catalogs of some 2,500 observed galaxies and nebulae. Later, when John traveled to the Cape Observatory in South Africa, he recorded another 1,700.

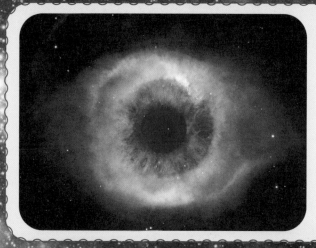

HELIX NEBULA

is located some 700 light-years away from Earth. It is the closest nebula to our planet. Looking at the nebula from Earth makes it appear like a bubble, but the shape is actually a cylinder pointed directly toward us.

BUTTERFLY NEBULA is named for its large, winglike shape—spanning over three light-years wide. The dying star that caused this nebula is very hot, which gives the wingspan temperatures of over 450,000°F. Scientists used the Hubble Space Telescope to capture an image of this nebula in 2009.

EAGLE NEBULA was discovered in 1745 by a Swiss astronomer named Jean-Philippe Loys de Chéseaux. Located 7,000 light-years away, Eagle Nebula features what is known as the "Pillars of Creation," a column-like region that spans 4 to 5 light-years, where stars are actively forming.

For those in the northern hemisphere, the ORION NEBULA can be spotted without a telescope and is best seen in January. Located south of the constellation Orion's Belt, it is the closest large star-forming region to Earth. The ancient Mayans thought of the Orion Nebula as a cosmic fire of creation.

Earth Layers

Earth is a rocky planet with four layers: an inner core, outer core, mantle, and crust.

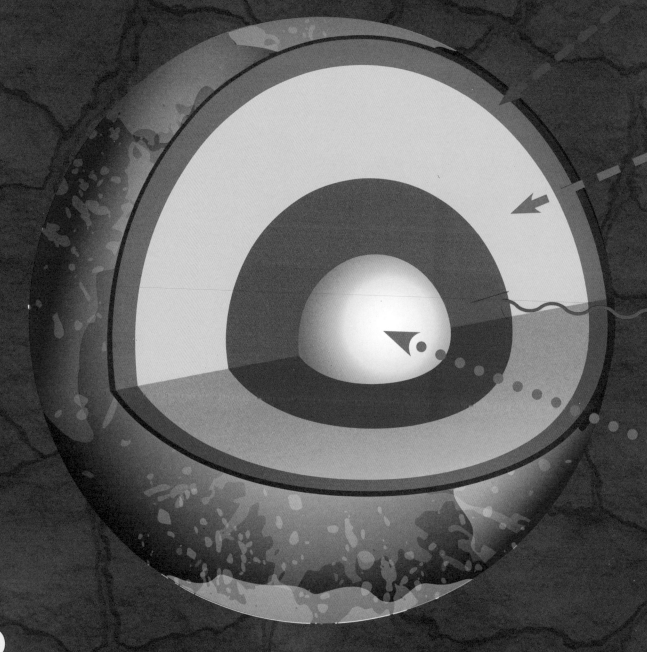

Atmosphere is the layer of air that surrounds Earth.

Crust is the top layer of rock and soil on Earth's surface. It is about 5 to 25 miles thick and goes down about 20 miles (that's about 5 miles beneath the oceans). This is the surface on which we live.

Mantle is the next layer, made of dense rock—some solid and some molten (melted). It is about 1,800 miles thick and 1,600°F to 4,000°F.

The outer core, made of molten iron (hot, liquid rock), is about 1,400 miles thick and is 4,000°F to 9,000°F.

The inner core is a ball of (extremely!) hot iron and nickel about 800 miles thick, around 12,000°F. Earth's center is the hottest place on the planet. It is solid, despite this heat, because the pressure of gravity is so great.

Hibernation

WHAT IS HIBERNATION?

A strategy to conserve energy when the weather is cold and food is scarce. Some animals such as black bears pass each winter curled up asleep in a warm place. Their body temperatures drop, and their body processes slow down.

HOW LONG CAN ANIMALS SURVIVE IN HIBERNATION?

Some animals hibernate for up to eight months. That's more than half the year!

What do the animals do for food?

Most animals eat huge amounts of food before they hibernate. This adds body fat and keeps them nourished during the winter months.

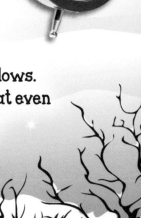

WHAT HAPPENS TO AN ANIMAL'S BODY IN HIBERNATION?

When an animal goes into hibernation, its temperature drops and its rate of breathing slows. It often goes into such a deep state of rest that even an alarm clock couldn't wake that animal up!

Are mammals the only animals that hibernate?

No. Although many mammals hibernate, some reptiles such as snakes and turtles hibernate, too. The box turtle hibernates and becomes so rested that its HEART only beats ONCE every FIVE TO 10 MINUTES. Instead of breathing, it takes in oxygen through its skin.

What do animals do when they hibernate?

Hibernating animals usually go into a den, burrow, or hollow log where they feel safe and warm. Then, they fall into a very deep and restful sleep. They don't even wake up to go to the bathroom!

What is a hibernating animal like when it wakes up in the spring?

HUNGry!

As soon as the animal wakes up, it goes hunting for food to fill its empty stomach.

Homes and Habitats

What is an organism?

Organisms are **LIVING CREATURES** that rely on one another for **SURVIVAL** in all places on Earth. For example, flowers need bees to pollinate them (spread their seeds), and bees need flowers to provide them with food. Nearly all species are interdependent, and each one contributes to its environment.

What are habitats?

The natural home of an animal or plant is called its habitat. A habitat has everything that an organism needs to survive: food, water, and shelter. A habitat is a specific place, such as a freshwater riverbed or the soggy floor of a tropical rain forest.

CAN HABITATS CHANGE?

Habitats can change. This can happen naturally or because humans have done something unnatural to bring it about.

Sometimes, a change in a habitat causes serious harm to the plants and animals that live there.

Maze

Outer Space

Most **NASA** expeditions to the International Space Station last about six months. See if you can navigate up, down, and around to find the correct pathway that takes the astronaut back to his spacecraft!

START

FINISH

Answers on page 313

Volcanoes

A **VOLCANO** is a large, MOUNTAIN-LIKE opening in the EARTH'S CRUST through which **MOLTEN LAVA** and GASES erupt.

Between the crust and the mantle is magma, which is made of rocks and gases. Magma is the liquid rock below Earth's surface. When two plates collide, magma is squeezed up between them, causing a volcanic eruption.

Earth's crust is made up of MOVABLE plates.

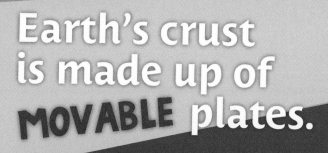

THE RING OF FIRE IS THE AREA THAT CIRCLES THE BASIN OF THE PACIFIC OCEAN, AND IT EARNED ITS NAME BECAUSE IT IS RESPONSIBLE FOR MOST OF THE WORLD'S VOLCANIC ERUPTIONS AND EARTHQUAKES!

LAVA IS THE LIQUID ROCK THAT FLOWS OUT OF THE VOLCANO.

Colors

HOW DO WE SEE COLORS?

The world is filled with colors. In order to see those colors, light is needed. Light is made of invisible waves, each in a different length. Each wavelength is a different color. When light from the sun hits Earth's atmosphere and scatters in many different directions, our eyes see different colors. The longest wavelength of light that human eyes can see is red; the shortest is blue.

WHAT IS THE COLOR SPECTRUM?

When light passes through a triangular glass called a prism, the glass bends the lights, splitting it into its different wavelengths. The light that comes out shows all the colors of the spectrum: red, orange, yellow, green, blue, indigo, and violet. The colors always appear in the same order.

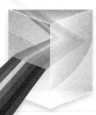

During the day, the blue parts of sunlight are scattered, so the sky looks blue. The rest of the light that gets through the atmosphere makes the sun look yellow/orange.

HOW CAN YOU REMEMBER THE COLORS OF THE SPECTRUM?

A handy way to remember the colors of the spectrum is to think of a guy name ROY G. BIV. The letters in his name stand for the colors in the proper order: red, orange, yellow, green, blue, indigo, and violet!

HELLO
my name is

Roy G. Biv

Word Search

Colors

Look at the puzzle below and see if you can find different types of colors and words relating to colors. Circle the words going across, up and down, and diagonally! Some words may be backward!

SPECTRUM	GREEN	WAVELENGTH
RED	BLUE	PRISM
ORANGE	COLOR	INDIGO
YELLOW	LIGHT	VIOLET

```
K P G E G X S V F L I R V M M
W R U R L V G D K J T U J U U
O L E D Z D I U O D J M Z I R
B E A L Q R O L O C P S O W T
N L M K J F P J Y M F I K F C
H I N P Q P M V O K L R Q H E
A T N M C K K I N U H P E C P
T J G D L U Q O E C U G X S S
S H O N I A E L A Y N R E D J
C S G W E G T E O A U K Z R H
P Q H I B L O T R Y C V X W S
S E S N L O E O D Q U C Z A C
Z A B T B A O V A V U C G E E
E O C E Y F H F A B G H A P E
Y E L L O W H F N W U D T H W
```

A Space for Music

On the International Space Station, astronauts are able to play musical instruments because of the microgravity and air inside. However, sometimes that microgravity means astronauts have to hold instruments differently—like strapping their feet down while playing a flute so that the tiny amount of air pushed out by blowing into it doesn't move them around.

Research is performed to determine the safety of bringing any material on board, including instruments. Guitars, for example, are made of wood, which means they are potentially flammable. Astronauts must take precautions like storing them away in special areas when they are not using them.

The first recorded song from space was in 1965 aboard *Gemini 6*. Bells and a harmonica were snuck onto the flight by astronauts Walter M. Schirra Jr. and Thomas P. Stafford, who played a joke on people listening at home on Earth by playing "Jingle Bells."

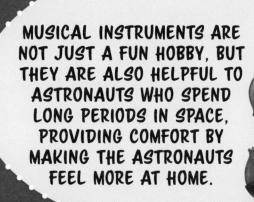

MUSICAL INSTRUMENTS ARE NOT JUST A FUN HOBBY, BUT THEY ARE ALSO HELPFUL TO ASTRONAUTS WHO SPEND LONG PERIODS IN SPACE, PROVIDING COMFORT BY MAKING THE ASTRONAUTS FEEL MORE AT HOME.

Instruments must be checked to ensure no gases are produced by their materials, as even a tiny amount could be disastrous in the contained environment of the space station. NASA tests this by putting items in a closed chamber and heating them for three days at as much as 120°F to measure potential toxins.

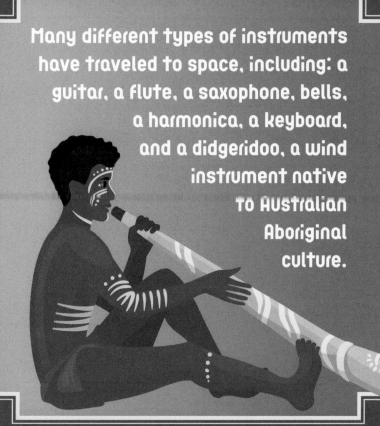

Many different types of instruments have traveled to space, including: a guitar, a flute, a saxophone, bells, a harmonica, a keyboard, and a didgeridoo, a wind instrument native to Australian Aboriginal culture.

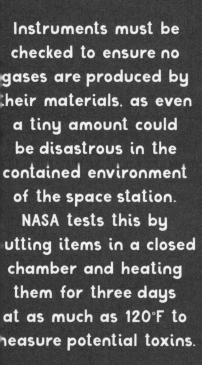

Word Scramble

Science

Unscramble the letters to spell out different branches of science.

The study of ancient people, societies, and cultures.

YARGLOCOEHA

__ __ __ __ __ __ __ __ __ __ __

The study of the origins and development of human beings.

ORHATNYGOLOP

__ __ __ __ __ __ __ __ __ __ __ __

The study of matter (anything you can see) and energy (movement) and how they interact.

SPHCISY

__ __ __ __ __ __ __

The study of living things.

GOLYBOI

__ __ __ __ __ __ __

A branch of biology that deals with plant life.

NAYOBT

__ __ __ __ __ __

The biological science that deals with the study of animals.

OOLZYGO

__ __ __ __ __ __ __

The branch of physics that studies the universe beyond Earth.

MONYORTAS

__ __ __ __ __ __ __ __ __

The science of preventing and curing diseases and injuries.

ENCIEDMI

__ __ __ __ __ __ __ __

The branch of natural sciences that deals with matter and the changes that take place within that matter.

MYISTRECH

__ __ __ __ __ __ __ __ __

Answers on page 315

Who Am I?

Scientists

Read the multiple choice questions below and choose the scientist who best fits the description.

1. **When you turn on the lights, think of me. I helped bring electricity to your home. Who am I?**

   a. Isaac Newton   b. Thomas Edison
   c. Charles Darwin d. Pythagoras

2. **Pasteurized milk is one of my claims to fame. Who am I?**

   a. Isaac Newton   b. Marie Curie
   c. Louis Pasteur   d. Albert Einstein

3. **I am responsible for the world's most famous equation, $E = mc^2$. Who am I?**

   a. Jane Goodall   b. Albert Einstein
   c. Alfred Nobel   d. Pythagoras

   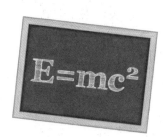

4. **Outstanding humanitarians receive an award in my name. Who am I?**

   a. Alfred Nobel   b. Marie Curie
   c. Pythagoras   d. Louis Pasteur

5. **The phonograph and movie projector are two of my most famous inventions. Who am I?**

   a. Alfred Nobel   b. Jane Goodall
   c. Thomas Edison   d. Stephen Hawking

6. **I've dedicated my life to studying and protecting the rights of animals. Who am I?**

   a. Marie Curie   b. Benjamin Franklin
   c. Louis Pasteur   d. Jane Goodall

7. **My invention, the telescope, has enabled scientists to study our solar system. Who am I?**

   a. Aristotle   b. Galileo Galilei
   c. Isaac Newton   d. Marie Curie

Famous Astronomers

Long ago, during the 2nd century CE, Claudius Ptolemy was an influential astronomer and mathematician. Though he inaccurately thought Earth to be the center of the universe, that belief led to his development of the Ptolemaic system, a mathematical model of the universe that greatly influenced those that followed. His writings on objects in the solar system, including his 13-book astronomical manual *Almagest*, were key resources to Greek astronomers.

ABD AL-RAHMAN AL-SUFI, OR AZOPHI, WAS AN IMPORTANT PERSIAN ASTRONOMER DURING THE 10TH CENTURY WHO TRANSLATED THE WRITTEN WORKS OF PTOLEMY AND VERIFIED THE ACCURACY OF THE CALCULATIONS. HE NOT ONLY MADE PTOLEMY'S CALCULATIONS MORE ACCURATE, BUT HE PREPARED HIS OWN DETAILED STAR CHARTS AND ILLUSTRATIONS. HIS WORK WAS CRUCIAL TO THE UNDERSTANDING OF CONSTELLATIONS, THE BRIGHTNESS OF STARS, AND GALAXIES.

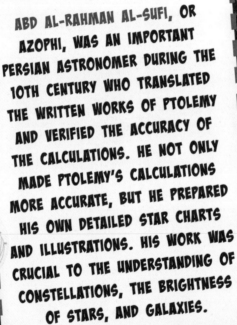

In the early 1500s, Nicolaus Copernicus, a Polish scientist, suggested that the planets in the solar system revolved around the sun. This was a controversial idea during his time, when most people believed that Earth was at the center of the universe. While Copernicus's calculations were not entirely correct, his ideas were foundational in the development of astronomical sciences.

English astronomer and mathematician **Edmond Halley** became the first person to calculate the orbit of a comet when he traced its path in the mid-1600s. Further research revealed that the same comet he spotted was seen at least four times before, leading him to calculate that the comet would again return in 1758. Though Halley died in 1742, the comet returned just as he predicted in 1758—which has since been renamed after him: Halley's Comet.

© Joe Sohm | Dreamstime.com

Carl Sagan was a popular American planetary scientist who made contributions to many different areas in astronomy. He consulted for NASA starting in the 1950s, when he spoke with astronauts right before their flights to the moon and helped design spacecrafts for missions to other planets. His interest in the possibility of extraterrestrial intelligence resulted in the Golden Record project. He wrote many books, created a television show called *Cosmos*, and made astronomy and difficult ideas about space and the planets easy for people to understand.

HENRIETTA SWAN LEAVITT discovered her interest in astronomy after college, despite not having formal training. She started volunteering at the Harvard College Observatory in 1895, and they hired her in 1902. There she discovered more than 2,400 variable stars, or stars that change from bright to dim. During her time, this was about half of all the variable stars discovered. She also helped develop photographic measurements for objects in space.

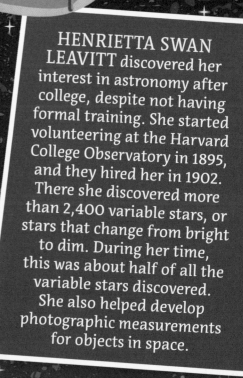

Tools of the Trade

Astronomers and Astronauts

The International Space Station has a 3D PRINTER, which made its first item in 2014: a plate engraved with the names of all the organizations that worked on the project. The printer gives astronauts the ability to build things they need while in space that they do not have access to, especially in case of a crisis.

Astronauts can use the pistol-grip tool, a cordless hand drill with an information screen, to make outside repairs to a spacecraft. It can withstand hundreds of degree changes in temperature and is light with a trigger-like design so it is comfortable for astronauts to use while wearing large, bulky space gloves.

The **TRACE GAS ANALYZER** is an essential tool to make sure there are no leaks of gas or fluid, such as rocket fuel or escaping oxygen, happening on a spacecraft. It is a small system, about the size of a shoebox, worn by an astronaut who can point it at areas they suspect may have a problem.

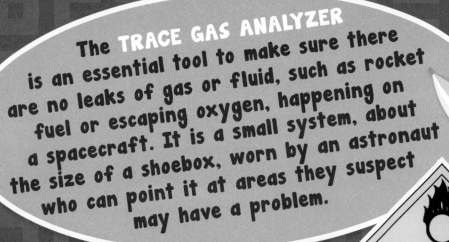

OXYGEN

2

THERE ARE TWO MAIN TYPES OF OPTICAL TELESCOPES: REFRACTORS AND REFLECTORS. REFRACTORS USE A GLASS LENS TO GATHER AND BEND LIGHT AND ARE THE FIRST TYPE OF TELESCOPE EVER DEVELOPED. REFLECTORS USE A MIRROR TO GATHER AND MAGNIFY LIGHT.

Early scientists used **astrolabes,** tools that would allow users to determine the placement of celestial objects at certain times and dates. The oldest date back to between 500 BC and 600 BC, and by the Middle Ages developed into portable, complex tools. They were inscribed brass discs, similar to pocket watches, with various levers and hands that could be moved to make calculations.

Electricity

In 1882, Thomas Edison opened the first power plant in New York City. In his plant, one big magnet rotated around a wire and produced an electric current. Today's power plants are bigger and controlled by computers, but the basic process remains the same—over 130 years later! Edison invented more than 2,000 products, including switches, fuses, sockets, and meters—all things we use in our homes every day.

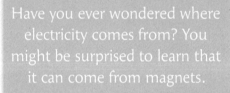

Have you ever wondered where electricity comes from? You might be surprised to learn that it can come from magnets.

How does solar energy work?

Solar collectors trap sunlight to generate (make) power. Solar cells turn the sun's energy into electricity. In places that get sunshine most of the year, solar panels are a cheaper, cleaner alternative to other power sources.

AMERICANS DOUBLE THEIR USE

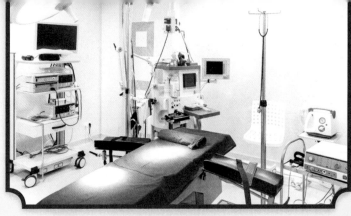

Wind can be used to make electricity.

Have you ever seen a windmill on a farm? When the wind turns the blades of a windmill, it spins a turbine inside a small generator to produce electricity, just like a big coal power plant.

ONLY 10% of energy in a standard LIGHT BULB is used to create light. Ninety percent of a light bulb's energy creates heat.

US HOSPITALS ARE SOME OF THE MOST ENERGY-INTENSE BUILDINGS ON THE PLANET.

WHAT IS HYDROELECTRIC ENERGY?

Hydroelectric energy, or hydroelectricity, is electricity made using the energy of falling water. *Hydro* means "water." About 9% of the electricity in the United States comes from hydroelectric sources.

OF ELECTRICITY EVERY 20 YEARS.

Migration

Migration refers to the movement of animal groups from one region to another, usually seasonally.

Just as hibernating animals seek warmth and protection from the cold winter months, migrating animals also look for a change from the cold, harsh season.

Scientists are not sure why some animals migrate, but most do so to find food or for breeding purposes.

Birds, mammals, reptiles, fish, and insects all migrate. Some migrate short distances, while others travel thousands of miles over a period of days to escape their winter homes.

Many crabs migrate to reproduce.

The African elephant migrates to find food during the wet and dry seasons.

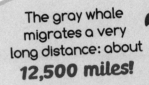

The gray whale migrates a very long distance: about **12,500 miles!**

The Baltimore oriole is a black and orange bird that migrates to find the fruit and nectar it likes to eat.

BATS ARE THE ONLY FLYING MAMMALS. SOME, LIKE THE RED BAT, MIGRATE FROM NORTH TO SOUTH.

The Arctic tern is a small bird that flies from the Arctic to the Antarctic and back again each year.

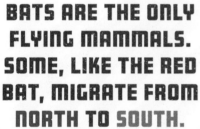

The nightingale, a small songbird, migrates and sings beautiful songs at night.

Frogs are amphibians that migrate back to the pond, marsh, or lake where they hatched as tadpoles, to lay their own eggs there.

THE TUNA IS A LARGE, BONY FISH THAT MIGRATES THOUSANDS OF MILES ACROSS THE OCEANS.

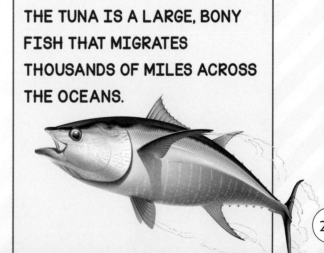

Natural Curiosities

Why do plants have thorns?
Why do cacti have needles?

It's a jungle out there, and plants have to defend themselves. Thorns and needles are the weapons of the plant world. Any animal that takes a bite out of a cactus is not coming back for a second helping!

What happens when water boils?

It disappears. Actually, at 212°F (100° Celsius), water changes to steam, which is a gas. All liquids become gases when heated to a certain point. Heat loosens the bonds between a liquid's molecules, and they spread apart, becoming a light, thin gas. At 32°F (0°C), water's molecules slow down and bind together into solid ice.

WHAT ARE SEASHELLS MADE OF?

"Skeletons." Many creatures without bones have exoskeletons—protective layers on the outside of their soft bodies. Some mollusks, like snails and clams, have exoskeletons made up mostly of calcium carbonate, the same substance found in limestone. No wonder shells are so hard! The shell is attached to the body, so once the mollusk dies, the shell is empty.

Where do Surinam toads incubate their eggs?

In the female toads' backs. A male fertilizes the eggs, then presses them into a female's back. Her skin covers the eggs until, after about 80 days, she sheds her skin. The tiny toads are then set free into the water.

Do sea horses swim the same way other fish do?

No. Unlike most fish, the sea horse swims in an upright position. It moves forward almost like a hummingbird, by flapping its tiny fins very fast—up to 35 times per second. Most fish use their tails to help them swim, but a sea horse uses its long, thin tail more like a hand than a fin. If a sea horse wants to stay in one spot for a while, it wraps its tail around seaweed or some other object and hangs on until it is ready to get going again.

HOW DO MALE SILK MOTHS FIND THEIR MATES?

By smell—and very well, too. The female silk moth gives off a tiny, tiny amount of scent. Experiments show that just one molecule of this substance is enough to alert a male moth to her presence. He can find her from more than a mile away!

Is there a reason why baby animals look so cute?

Scientists think that the big eyes of many baby animals let adult animals know that the youngsters are harmless and need care. Some baby animals have special markings, making adult animals less likely to chase them away, as they would if adult animals entered the same territory.

Tropical Rain Forest

You've just entered a beautiful, lush jungle filled with unusual flowers, animals, and birds, enormous plants and trees, and green all around. Though it rains at least 10 times more here than in other parts of the world, you'll only need a light jacket with a hood. The temperatures range from a comfortable 70°F to a high of around 90°F, day or night, all year round.

The Layers of the Rain Forest

1. EMERGENT: This is where the tallest trees grow higher than the canopy, sticking up above it.

2. CANOPY: This is the upper layer of the forest, where leaves and branches grow close together and form a layer high above the forest floor. The canopy is full of bird and animal life.

3. UNDERSTORY: This is the rain forest layer where trees are below the canopy. Many species of plants and animals can be found in the understory layer.

4. FOREST FLOOR: This is the bottom layer of the rain forest—where most insects and animals crawl—that includes the ground. Only plants that don't need sun grow here.

Animals of the Tropical Rain Forest

Many animals make their home in the tropical rain forest. Below are just a few.

ORANGUTANS

These large apes live in the trees of the Southeast Asian tropical rain forest. They eat fruit, leaves, flowers, and vines.

MONARCH BUTTERFLIES

Mainly found in North America, these butterflies are actually poisonous! Predators avoid eating them because they become sick from the poison.

Poison dart frogs

These tiny frogs advertise that they are poisonous with their brightly colored skin so predators don't eat them. They catch their diet of insects and spiders using their great vision and sticky tongues.

Jaguars

Wild cats of Central and South America, jaguars are nocturnal animals that hunt turtles, birds, and reptiles in the rain forest.

CAPYBARAS

These rodents are great swimmers. They have webbed feet and like to eat aquatic plants, tree bark, and fruits of the rain forest.

Extinction

Extinction is a natural part of life. New species develop and others become extinct. In modern times, species are dying out more rapidly than they did in the past. Why?

HUNTING ANIMALS FOR THEIR MEAT OR FUR CAN BE DEVASTATING TO A SPECIES.

Deforestation, or destruction of the forest, is a major cause of extinction. This means that humans are cutting down trees in forests where animals live and eat to build homes and other developments. Deforestation can also happen through natural disasters like floods, fires, and drought.

Removing animals from their natural environments and using them for entertainment or bringing them into homes as pets can add to the destruction of a species.

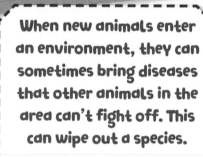

When new animals enter an environment, they can sometimes bring diseases that other animals in the area can't fight off. This can wipe out a species.

Humans destroy the natural environment of a living thing when they fill swamps and marshes and dam rivers for new home and building developments.

Oil spills, acid rain, and water pollution can destroy fish and bird populations.

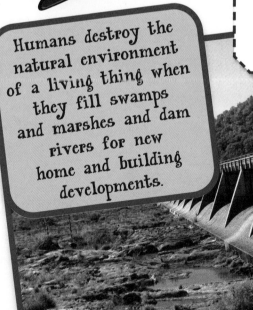

Spot the Difference
Tropical Rain Forest

Rain forests are the oldest of the planet's ecosystems. On average, 137 different life forms and species are driven to extinction on a daily basis in the tropical rain forest, particularly due to deforestation.

Find and circle 6 differences between these two pictures of rain forests.

Dinosaur Timeline

What are the Time Periods of the DINOSAURS?

The MESOZOIC ERA, which is often referred to as the *AGE OF DINOSAURS*, is the time period between 251 million years ago until around 65 million years ago in which dinosaurs existed. This era is broken down into three separate time periods: the Triassic Period, Jurassic Period, and Cretaceous Period. It is at the end of the Cretaceous Period that dinosaurs became extinct.

TRIASSIC PERIOD
(about 251 to 199 million years ago)

JURASSIC PERIOD
(about 199 to 145 million years ago)

CRETACEOUS PERIOD
(about 145 to 65 million years ago)

Fun Fact
Humans have only been on Earth for 6 million years!

Look at your arm. Imagine that life on Earth began at your shoulder. The dinosaurs were around from below your elbow to your wrist. Humans have been here only for the little bit of time represented by the tip of one fingernail!

Iguanodon

Iguanodon had a toothless beak, so how did it grind up the tough plants it liked to eat? Unlike other dinosaurs, *Iguanodon* had strong teeth (about 2 inches long) in the sides of its jaw. These cheek teeth ground up tough plant material.

DID YOU KNOW?

The *Iguanodon*'s hind legs were longer than its front legs. Although it generally walked on all four legs, *Iguanodon* was able to easily stand on its two hind legs.

Iguanodon had two cone-shaped spikes, one on each of its front claws. Paleontologists believe these spikes—known as thumb spikes—may have been used for sparring or to fight off enemies.

Where Did All the Dinosaurs Go?

Dinosaurs, along with many other animals, roamed Earth for millions of years. Then, at the end of the Cretaceous Period, they died out, or became extinct. Scientists have many different theories about this mass extinction. Here are just a couple of ideas:

VOLCANO Theory

Millions of years ago, there was a great deal of volcanic activity in India. This could have caused massive changes in climate, making it hard for plants and animals—including dinosaurs—to survive.

BOOM!

ASTEROID THEORY

Many scientists believe a massive asteroid hit Earth about 65 million years ago. The impact from the asteroid would have caused great damage and changes in the atmosphere, killing plants and animals. This means that plant-eating dinosaurs and animals would eventually starve to death because of changes in the climate from dust clouds in the atmosphere.

Earth's Major Biomes

DESERT

An extremely dry region that is usually hot. Some species of plants and animals that live in deserts include the Saguaro cactus, sagebrush, camels, scorpions, Gila monsters, kangaroos, and rattlesnakes.

Forest

A land area covered with trees and underbrush. There are several different types of forest, including temperate forests, boreal forests, and rain forests. The types of animals living in a forest depend on the area's climate and types of trees growing there.

A region where grasses are the main form of plant life. There are different types of grasslands, including savannas, found in tropical areas, and temperate grasslands, found in cool-weather areas. Grassland areas include scrublands, where small trees and shrubs grow, as well as grasses. The types of animals living in these areas vary, depending on the climate.

GRASSLAND

TUNDRA

An area too cold for trees to grow. Mosses, lichens, and some flowering plants grow there. Musk oxen, caribou, ermine, walruses, arctic foxes, and polar bears are some animals that live in tundra areas.

ALPINE

A mountainous area that might shelter yaks, snow leopards, mountain goats, pikas, eagles, or bighorn sheep.

OCEAN

The world's largest biome. Its huge variety of plant and animal life includes the remora fish, lobsters, stingrays, sharks, seals, octopuses, corals, and seaweed.

Forecast Says

What happens to a mercury thermometer at -40°F and below?

It becomes useless because the mercury freezes. To measure temperatures colder than -40°F, scientists use thermometers filled with alcohol, or ones that measure the movement of electrons.

Why does it take longer to hard-boil an egg in Denver than in New Orleans?

Water's boiling point is strongly affected by air pressure, which is lower at high altitudes. Water boils at a lower temperature because of the lower atmospheric pressure. That's why you need more time to boil an egg in Denver, Colorado—nicknamed "the Mile High City" for its high altitude—than in New Orleans, Louisiana, which is at sea level.

$$(32°F - 32) \times 5 \div 9$$

What is the difference between Fahrenheit and Celsius temperatures?

Fahrenheit (F) and Celsius (C) are two different scales that give the same information: the temperature in degrees. Water freezes at a certain temperature: 32°F or 0°C. Its boiling point is 212°F or 100°C. To convert from Fahrenheit to Celsius, take the temperature, subtract 32, multiply by 5, then divide by 9. To convert Celsius to Fahrenheit, multiply the Celsius temperature by 1.8, then add 32.

15° 70°

How quickly can the temperature change?

Ask anyone who was in Spearfish, South Dakota, on January 22, 1943. That day, the temperature in Spearfish shot up 49 degrees in just two minutes (from -4°F to 45°F). Later that same morning, it fell 58 degrees (from 54°F to -4°F) in 27 minutes! That weather roller coaster was probably caused by cold and warm fronts bouncing off the Black Hills and across the Great Plains.

How do paleoclimatologists figure out Earth's past climates?

They use many kinds of clues. Ancient air trapped in Antarctica's ice gives information about the atmosphere long ago. Plant and animal fossils can reveal how warm, cold, wet, or dry it was in the past. Experts called palynologists even study pollen, ancient and modern. By figuring out what plant the tiny fossilized grains came from, palynologists can reconstruct ancient landscapes.

WHERE WAS THE FIRST REAL WEATHER-RECORDING STATION?

Oxford, England. The Radcliffe Observatory there began keeping regular daily weather records in January 1815, tracking the area's temperature and rainfall. The Radcliffe's archives include older weather records; irregular readings were taken there as far back as 1767.

Animal Facts

How do moles live underground?

They constantly dig tunnels with their strong front claws searching for tasty worms and grubs to eat. The tunnels also connect them to underground nests and resting places. Their molehills, the excess earth from all that digging, have ruined many a lawn.

How and why do CHAMELEONS change color?

It's hide-and-seek in the animal world every day. Some animals hide while others seek to eat them. The chameleon has a natural ability to hide by changing its colors to match its surroundings. If it stays long enough in one spot, its color cells will change to blend in with the background. They also change color when it's too hot or cold, or if they feel threatened.

WHAT IS OCTOPUS INK?

It's a smoke screen. When threatened, an octopus discharges a thick blackish or brownish inky fluid that is stored in its body. The ejected ink doesn't dissolve quickly. It floats in the water in a cloud shaped somewhat like an octopus. The idea is to confuse the octopus's enemies and cover its escape—and it works.

Why do beavers build dams?

They're building homes. The amazing beaver "lodge" is a marvel of animal architecture. Beavers begin by cutting down trees with their sharp front teeth and powerful jaws. They use the tree trunks to build a watertight dam in a pond or lake. The dam is used to decrease the water level and to widen their living space. Then they build a room with rocks and twigs plastered together with mud. There's even a hole in the floor leading to the pond. Inside, beavers sleep and raise families.

Are all snakes poisonous?

No. Snakes have a bad reputation because of the few poisonous ones. Of the 2,700 snake species, only about 400 are poisonous. Fewer than 50 kinds are dangerous to people. Most snakes will avoid people if at all possible. The anaconda, weighing more than 500 pounds, is not poisonous but can squeeze the life out of a crocodile.

Why do monkeys and apes groom each other?

Why do humans shake hands or give hugs? Touching is a form of communication. A social act, grooming helps to keep a group of monkeys together. Grooming is also symbolic of a monkey's social status. A monkey grooms those with a higher social position and is groomed by those of lower rank. Above all, grooming keeps apes and monkeys clean!

WHAT MAKES A SKUNK SMELL?

The ghastly spray is the skunk's best defense and, boy, does it work! No creature, human, or beast can stand being near a skunk with that odor. It comes from a fluid called musk, which is produced and stored in a pair of glands under the animal's tail. A skunk can propel its spray about 10 feet!

HOW BIG IS A BABY WHALE?

Bigger than any other baby on Earth. The largest whale is the blue whale, and its baby is the biggest. At birth, these babies can be 20 to 26 feet long and weigh more than 6,000 pounds. Just one year later, they can grow to be 28 tons!

This and That

Who invented chewing gum?

The stuff of chewing gum is chicle (CHEE-clay), the gum of the sapodilla tree. The Aztec Indians of Mexico chewed it to clean their teeth. In 1872, Thomas Adams mixed sugar and flavor with chicle and created a rubbery candy. Actually, he was looking for a substitute for rubber when he popped a piece of chicle into his mouth. He chewed on his idea for a while and out popped gum!

What makes a flower smell good?

All plants and animals have characteristics or behaviors that help them reproduce. In order to grow seeds, flowers must transfer pollen from their male parts to their female parts. Insects often carry the pollen, and flowers attract insects with their smells. The perfume comes from tiny particles, called scent strips, on the petals and other parts of the flowers.

WHO INVENTED GUNPOWDER?

The Chinese. It was originally meant for fireworks, not for guns. It was invented around 1000 AD and was probably a result of experiments attempting to turn chemicals and other substances into gold. Later, the Chinese used the explosive on the tips of arrows for rocketlike weapons. By the 1200s, gun powder was used by Europeans as well.

Why did Congress pass the Endangered Species Act?

To protect plants and animals threatened by human activities. This law, passed in 1973, makes any activity that threatens the survival of an endangered species illegal. In North America alone, more than 900 plants and animals are considered endangered.

ENDANGERED
SPECIES

Who was Charles Darwin?

Charles Darwin (1809-1882) was a naturalist (a scientist who studies the natural world). In 1859, he published *Origin of Species*, a book that presented the theory of evolution—the idea that all plant and animal life gradually change in form, adapting to suit their environments. Darwin's ideas caused a major shift in how people viewed the world, and sparked debates that continue to this day.

WHERE IS THE WORLD'S LONGEST CAVE?

Mammoth Cave National Park in Kentucky. Since finding a passageway between Mammoth Cave and the Flint Ridge cave system, explorers have discovered over 400 miles of cave trails—and counting!

Page 23

Word Search

Super Solar System

Pretend you are an astronomer and look for the planets and space-themed words in the puzzle below. Circle the words going across, up and down, and diagonally. Some words may be backward!

ASTEROIDS	JUPITER	NEPTUNE	SATURN
COMETS	MARS	ORBIT	SPACE
EARTH	MERCURY	PLANETS	URANUS
GRAVITY	MOON	PLUTO	VENUS

Page 27

Word Search
Prehistoric Hunt

A paleontologist is a scientist who studies fossils and bones to learn about dinosaurs and other prehistoric life. Pretend you are a paleontologist and hunt for the following prehistoric creatures in the puzzle below. Circle the words going across, up and down, and diagonally. Some words may be backward!

ALLOSAURUS	MEGALOSAURUS	SPINOSAURUS
APATOSAURUS	MOSASAURUS	STEGOSAURUS
BRACHIOSAURUS	PLESIOSAURUS	TRICERATOPS
IGUANODON	PTERANODON	VELOCIRAPTOR

Answers

Fill-in Puzzle
Geology Genius

The word "crystal" comes from various root words, including the Greek *kryos* for "frost." Ancient peoples thought rock crystals were ice that was so frozen it would never thaw.

Use the words at the bottom of the page to fill in the blanks in the puzzle.

Puzzle grid answers:

```
                    S
              G     L
              O     A
              L     T
        S E D I M E N T A R Y
        E
  M     D
  A S   I
  G R A N I T E
  M A   M
L A V A D
        E
  M O U N T A I N
  V     N   G
  O     T   N
  L     M E T A M O R P H I C
S T O N E   O
  A     P U M I C E
  O         U
            S
```

4 Letters	5 Letters	6 Letters	7 Letters	8 Letters	11 Letters
Sand	Magma	Pumice	Igneous	Mountain	Sedimentary
Lava	Stone		Volcano	Sediment	Metamorphic
Gold	Slate		Granite		

Page 79

Crack the Code

Man on the Moon

Solve the cryptogram below to reveal what Neil Armstrong famously said on July 20, 1969, when he became the first human on the moon. Use the key below to fill in the blanks and reveal the quote.

1=A	5=W	9=E	13=M	17=D	21=X	25=R
2=B	6=V	10=L	14=Z	18=K	22=C	26=P
3=S	7=T	11=G	15=Y	19=I	23=Q	
4=J	8=F	12=O	16=H	20=N	24=U	

"T H A T ' S   O N E   S M A L L
7 16 1 7 3   12 20 9   3 13 1 10 10

S T E P   F O R   M A N,
3 7 9 26   8 12 25   13 1 20'

O N E   G I A N T   L E A P
12 20 9   11 19 1 20 7   10 9 1 26

F O R   M A N K I N D."
8 12 25   13 1 20 18 19 20 17

Neil Armstrong always loved to fly. He got his pilot's license at 16 years old, even before his driver's license! He went to college, served as a Navy pilot, and then worked for NASA as a test pilot—where he learned to fly over 200 different aircrafts. It's no wonder this career-flyer then acted as mission commander on Apollo 11: the first mission to the moon.

Page 99

Crazy Maze
Velociraptor

Small and lightweight, *Velociraptor* was very fast. Sometimes known as the "speedy thief," this dinosaur could quickly steal food from other animals. *Velociraptor* is on the hunt for delicious eggs for breakfast. Help it find its way through the maze to find the nest.

START

FINISH

Answers

Search & Find®
Laboratory

From Aristotle to Charles Darwin to Neil deGrasse Tyson, scientists over the centuries have used tools and equipment to conduct research and experiments in their laboratories. Even though modern labs rely on computer technology, some tools, like mortar and pestle, have been around since the Stone Age!

Search & Find® these 6 types of tools and equipment in the science laboratory below.

Microscope

Bunsen burner

Test tubes

Computer

Scale

Mortar and pestle

Page 121

Crossword Puzzle
Essential Vitamins

Complete the crossword using the clues below. For help, use the information you've learned about essential vitamins.

ACROSS

2. Eating carrots and other vegetables with vitamin A helps keep my _____ clear.

3. This orange food is a popular Halloween decoration and loaded with vitamin A.

4. Drinking a glass of _____ juice in the morning will give me vitamin C.

6. Raisin _____ is a cereal rich in vitamin B3.

DOWN

1. Drinking _____ may help my body to stop bleeding after a bad fall.

2. This is the fruit of a flower and very rich in vitamin E. _____ seed.

3. A _____ butter and jelly sandwich is yummy and packed with vitamin E.

5. An _____ and cheese sandwich is a good breakfast to provide vitamin B2.

Answers

Spot the Difference
Spacecrafts

The Space Shuttle was a specific spacecraft that NASA operated from 1981 to 2011. The shuttle flew 135 missions, including transporting crew to build the International Space Station. The Space Shuttle is no longer used because of some limitations in the design: space travel was limited to two weeks and no farther than low Earth orbit. As scientists seek to explore deeper into space, they must create new vehicles able to withstand that journey.

Find and circle six things that are different between the two spacecrafts.

Page 149

Word Scramble

Wild About Weather

Every year there are about 16 million thunderstorms, which means that there are around 2,000 thunderstorms happening every minute!

Unscramble the letters to spell out different weather terms.

AIPRODSNR
R A I N D R O P S

GILHIGTNN
L I G H T N I N G

CDLUSO
C L O U D S

NUEICAHRR
H U R R I C A N E

NDOOTAR
T O R N A D O

ALHI
H A I L

UHRDENT
T H U N D E R

BRLZADIZ
B L I Z Z A R D

DIWN
W I N D

NWSO
S N O W

Answers

Page 161

Crack the Code
National Park Pride

Solve the cryptogram below to reveal a famous quote from John Muir. Use the key below to fill in the blanks and reveal the quote.

1=S	5=F	9=H	13=R	17=V	21=O	25=M
2=D	6=K	10=B	14=I	18=C	22=G	26=Z
3=U	7=Q	11=N	15=A	19=L	23=Y	
4=E	8=P	12=W	16=T	20=X	24=J	

"THE MOUNTAINS
16 9 4 25 21 3 11 16 15 14 11 1

ARE CALLING
15 13 4 18 15 19 19 14 1! 22

AND I MUST GO."
15 11 2 14 25 3 1 16 22 21

Considered by many in the United States as the "Father of our National Parks," John Muir was an early naturalist and conservationist. He founded the Sierra Club, a California wildlife conservation organization, and his writings to the US government contributed to the protection of many natural areas: the Grand Canyon, Sequoia National Park, Mount Rainier, and Yosemite.

©iStock.com/PictureLake

307

Page 181

Making Words

Aquatic Wordsmith

There are many different types of bodies of water. Here are just a few: A SPRING is water that flows from underground up to the surface; a CREEK is a small stream; a BAYOU is slow-moving water with marshy vegetation, or plants; a TRIBUTARY is a stream that flows into a larger stream or river; and a MEANDER is a bend in a winding river.

Look at the word below. How many words, of three or more letters, can you make using only the letters in MEANDER? Fill out your answers on the lines below.

MEANDER

Here are words you might have made:

EARNED	DEAR
NEARED	EARN
REAMED	MADE
REMADE	MANE
AMEND	MEAN
ARMED	MEND
DREAM	NAME
EARED	NEAR
NAMED	NEED
DARE	READ

Page 199

Word Search
Mammals

Look for different kinds of mammals in the puzzle below. Circle the words going across, up and down, and diagonally. Some words may be backward!

ANTELOPE	GORILLA	POLAR BEAR
BUFFALO	HEDGEHOG	RHINOCEROS
DOLPHIN	LEOPARD	WEASEL
ELEPHANT	ORANGUTAN	ZEBRA

```
N V A G S V N B T R X S H R E
A E R Z D O U C A S I O E J I
T O X I R F R E E N O I D L I
U N F R F E B E O R Y U G A D
G W S A I R U M C E I A E N R
N H L N A X M P G O D V H W A
A O W L Z E B R A D N M O I P
R P O X U Y L A L L T I G W O
O P O D G L R E M B L I H L E
U U Y W Y F H E P S A I E R L
N I H P L O D I M H N S R Y O
F C R C O M H F T P A R F O F
U A J L P R O N H E U N E U G
S M Y O G H U O W Z I E T H X
J W A N T E L O P E U V L B R
```

Making Words

Inter-speller

The word "planet" comes from various root words, including the Greek asters *planetai*, or "wandering stars."

Look at the word below. How many words, of three or more letters, can you make using only the letters in PLANET? Fill out your answers on the lines below.

PLANET

Here are words you might have made:

LANE	PLANE
LATE	PLANT
LEAN	PLATE
LEAP	TALE
NEAT	TAPE
PALE	ATE
PEAL	EAT
PLAN	LAP
PANE	LET
PETAL	PEA

Underwater Matching
Fishy Trio

The Great Barrier Reef, located off the coast of Australia, is the world's largest reef system, made up of 900 islands and over 2,900 individual reefs. Many different species of animals live there, including 215 species of birds, 17 species of sea snakes, 30 species of whales, dolphins, and porpoises, and over 1,500 species of fish.

There are many different types of fish under the sea! Look at the underwater scene and circle the 3 fish that are exactly the same.

Answers

Fill-in Puzzle
Photosynthesis Phonics

Why do leaves change colors—reds, yellows, and oranges—in the fall? As the seasons change, temperatures get cooler and daylight decreases, which causes trees to produce less chlorophyll. With less chlorophyll, and eventually none at all, the other pigments in the leaf become visible—leading to an array of vibrant autumn colors. Climate change is impacting the changing leaves, as changes to precipitation and temperature impact the length of the colorful fall season.

Use the words at the bottom of the page to fill in the blanks in the puzzle.

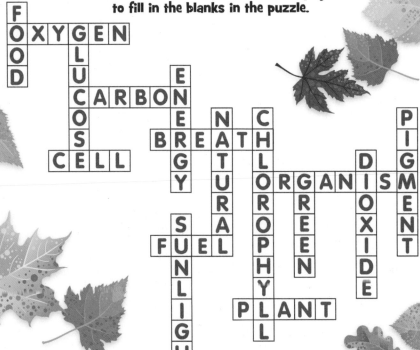

4 Letters	5 Letters	6 Letters	7 Letters	8 Letters	11 Letters
Food	Green	Oxygen	Pigment	Organism	Chlorophyll
Fuel	Plant	Energy	Natural	Sunlight	
Cell		Carbon	Dioxide		
		Breath	Glucose		

Answers

Maze

Outer Space

Most **NASA** expeditions to the International Space Station last about six months. See if you can navigate up, down, and around to find the correct pathway that takes the astronaut back to his spacecraft!

START

FINISH

Word Search

Colors

Look at the puzzle below and see if you can find
different types of colors and words relating to colors.
Circle the words going across, up and down, and
diagonally! Some words may be backward!

SPECTRUM	GREEN	WAVELENGTH
RED	BLUE	PRISM
ORANGE	COLOR	INDIGO
YELLOW	LIGHT	VIOLET

Answers

Word Scramble
Science

Unscramble the letters to spell out different branches of science.

The study of ancient people, societies, and cultures.

YARGLOCOEHA
A R C H A E O L O G Y

The study of the origins and development of human beings.

ORHATNYGOLOP
A N T H R O P O L O G Y

The study of matter (anything you can see) and energy (movement) and how they interact.

SPHCISY
P H Y S I C S

The study of living things.

GOLYBOI
B I O L O G Y

A branch of biology that deals with plant life.

NAYOBT
B O T A N Y

The biological science that deals with the study of animals.

OOLZYGO
Z O O L O G Y

The branch of physics that studies the universe beyond Earth.

MONYORTAS
A S T R O N O M Y

The science of preventing and curing diseases and injuries.

ENCIEDMI
M E D I C I N E

The branch of natural sciences that deals with matter and the changes that take place within that matter.

MYISTRECH
C H E M I S T R Y

Answers

Who Am I?

Scientists

Read the multiple choice questions below and choose the scientist who best fits the description.

1. When you turn on the lights, think of me. I helped bring electricity to your home. Who am I?
   a. Isaac Newton   (b. Thomas Edison)
   c. Charles Darwin d. Pythagoras

2. Pasteurized milk is one of my claims to fame. Who am I?
   a. Isaac Newton   b. Marie Curie
   (c. Louis Pasteur) d. Albert Einstein

3. I am responsible for the world's most famous equation, E = mc². Who am I?
   a. Jane Goodall   (b. Albert Einstein)
   c. Alfred Nobel   d. Pythagoras

$$E=mc^2$$

4. Outstanding humanitarians receive an award in my name. Who am I?
   (a. Alfred Nobel)   b. Marie Curie
   c. Pythagoras   d. Louis Pasteur

5. The phonograph and movie projector are two of my most famous inventions. Who am I?
   a. Alfred Nobel   b. Jane Goodall
   (c. Thomas Edison) d. Stephen Hawking

6. I've dedicated my life to studying and protecting the rights of animals. Who am I?
   a. Marie Curie   b. Benjamin Franklin
   c. Louis Pasteur   (d. Jane Goodall)

7. My invention, the telescope, has enabled scientists to study our solar system. Who am I?
   a. Aristotle   (b. Galileo Galilei)
   c. Isaac Newton   d. Marie Curie

Answers

Spot the Difference
Tropical Rain Forest

Rain forests are the oldest of the planet's ecosystems. On average, 137 different life forms and species are driven to extinction on a daily basis in the tropical rain forest, particularly due to deforestation.

Find and circle 6 differences between these two pictures of rain forests.